THE **TESTING** SERIES

RAF AIRMAN
TEST

THE **TESTING** SERIES
expert advice on test preparation

how2become

Orders: Please contact How2become Ltd, Suite 2, 50 Churchill Square Business Centre, Kings Hill, Kent ME19 4YU.

Telephone: (44) 0845 643 1299 - Lines are open Monday to Friday 9am until 5pm. Fax: (44) 01732 525965. You can also order via the e-mail address info@ how2become.co.uk.

ISBN: 9781909229914

First published 2013

Typeset for How2become Ltd by Molly Hill, Canada.

Printed in Great Britain for How2become Ltd by Bell & Bain Ltd, 303 Burnfield Road, Thornliebank, Glasgow G46 7UQ.

CONTENTS

INTRODUCTION

Dear Sir/Madam,

Welcome to your new guide, RAF Airman Tests: Practice Tests for the Royal Air Force. This guide contains hundreds of sample test questions that are appropriate for anyone who is applying to join the RAF as an Airman/Airwoman.

The selection tests for the RAF are designed to assess potential employees 'suitability' for specific posts. In the majority of cases, the higher scores you achieve, the more job opportunities you will have at your disposal. The key to success is to try your hardest to get 100% correct answers in the test that you are undertaking. If you aim for 100% in your preparation, then you are far more likely to achieve the trade or career that you want. We have deliberately supplied you with lots of sample questions to assist you. It is crucial that when you get a question wrong, you take the time to find out why you got it wrong. Understanding the question is very important.

Finally, if you want to try out more tests that will prepare you for the RAF then we offer a wide range of products to assist you at www.how2become.com.

Good luck and best wishes,

The how2become team

The How2become team

PREFACE BY AUTHOR RICHARD McMUNN

It's probably important that I start off by explaining a little bit about myself, my background, and also why I'm suitably qualified to help you pass the selection tests that form part of the Royal Air Force.

At the time of writing I am 41 years old and live in Tunbridge Wells, Kent. I left school at the usual age of 16 and joined the Royal Navy, serving on-board HMS Invincible as part of 800 Naval Air Squadron which formed part of the Fleet Air Arm. There I was at the age of 16, travelling the world and working as an engineer on Sea Harrier jets! It was fantastic and I loved every minute of it. After four years I left the Royal Navy and joined Kent Fire and Rescue Service as a firefighter. Over the next 17 years I worked my way up through the ranks to the position of Assistant Divisional Officer. During my time in the Fire Service I spent a lot of time working as an instructor at the Fire Brigade Training Centre. I was also involved in the selection process for assessing candidates who wanted to join the job as a firefighter. Therefore, my knowledge and experience gained so far in life has been invaluable in helping people like you to pass any type of selection process. I am sure you will find this guide an invaluable resource during your preparation for joining the Royal Air Force.

I have always been fortunate in the fact that I persevere at everything I do. I've understand that if I keep working hard in life then I will always be successful; or I will achieve whatever it is that I want to achieve. This is an important lesson that I want you to take on-board straight away. If you work hard and persevere, then success will come your way. The same rule applies whilst applying for a career in the Armed Forces; if you work hard and try lots of test questions, then you will be successful.

Finally, it is very important that you believe in your own abilities. It does not matter if you have no qualifications. It does not matter if are currently weak in the area of psychometric testing. What does matter is self-belief, self-discipline and a genuine desire to improve and become successful.

Best wishes,

Richard McMunn

DISCLAIMER

TIPS FOR PASSING THE RAF AIRMAN TESTS

There's no two ways about it, the most effective way in which you can prepare for the tests is to carry out lots of sample test questions. When I say lots, I mean lots!

Before I provide you with a host of test questions for you to try, here are a few important tips for you to consider:

- It is important that, before you sit your test, you find out the type(s) of test you will be required to undertake. You should also take steps to find out if the tests will be timed and also whether or not they will be 'multiple-choice' based questions. If the tests that you will be required to undertake are timed and of multiple-choice in nature, then I strongly advise that you practice this type of test question.

- Variety is the key to success. I recommend that you attempt a variety of different test questions, such as numerical reasoning, verbal reasoning, fault analysis, spatial reasoning and mechanical reasoning etc. This will undoubtedly improve your overall ability to pass the test that you are required to undertake.

- Confidence is an important part of test preparation. Have you ever sat a timed test and your mind goes blank? This is because your mind is focused on negative thoughts and your belief that you will fail the test. If you practice plenty of test questions under timed conditions then your confidence will grow. If your confidence is at its peak at the commencement of the test then there is no doubt that you will actually look forward to sitting it, as opposed to being fearful of the outcome.

- Whilst this is a very basic tip that may appear obvious, many people neglect to follow it. Make sure that you get a good night's sleep the night before your RAF Airman test or assessment. Research has shown that those people who have regular 'good' sleep are far more likely to concentrate better during psychometric tests.

- Try practicing numerical test questions in your head, without writing down your workings out. This is very difficult to accomplish, but it is excellent practice for the real test. Also, practice numerical reasoning tests without a calculator. If you are permitted to use a calculator at the test, make sure you know how to use one!

- You are what you eat! In the week prior to the test eat and drink healthily. Avoid cigarettes, alcohol and food with high fat content. The reason for this is that all of these will make you feel sluggish and you will not perform at your peak. On the morning of your assessment eat a healthy breakfast such as porridge and a banana.

- Drink plenty of water, always!

- If you have any special needs that need to be catered for ensure you inform the assessment centre staff prior to the assessment day. I have met people in the past who are fearful of telling the assessment staff that they are dyslexic. You will not be treated negatively; in fact the exact opposite. They will give you extra time in the tests which can only work in your favour.

Now that I have provided you with a number of important tips, take the time to work through the many different sample test questions that are contained within the guide. You will need a stop watch in order to assess your performance against the time constraints for each test.

CHAPTER 1
ABOUT THE ROYAL AIR FORCE AIRMAN/ AIRWOMAN TEST

Before we get into some sample practice questions for the Royal Air Force Selection Test (AST), let's first recap on what the test actually involves.

The AST consists of a number of different aptitude tests, which are designed to assess which careers in the RAF you are most suited to. There are many different career opportunities available and each one requires a different level of skill. The AST consists of seven timed multiple choice aptitude tests as follows:

- A verbal reasoning test which assesses how well you can interpret written information. During this test you will have 15 minutes to answer 20 questions;

- A numerical reasoning test which determines how accurately you can interpret numerical information such as charts, graphs and tables. The test will also assess your ability to use fractions, decimals and different formula. There are two parts to this test. During the first test you will have just 4 minutes to answer 12 questions that are based on fractions, decimals and formula. During the second test you will have 11 minutes to answer 15 questions that relate to different graphs and tables;

- A work rate test which is used to assess how quickly and accurately you can carry out routine tasks. During this test you will have 4 minutes to answer 20 questions;

- A spatial reasoning test designed to examine your ability to work with different shapes and objects. During this test you will have just 4 minutes to answer 10 questions;

- A mechanical comprehension test which is used to assess how effectively you can work with different mechanical concepts. During this particular test you will have 10 minutes in which to answer 20 questions;

- An electrical comprehension test which will assess your ability to work with different electrical concepts. During this test you will have 11 minutes to complete 21 questions.

- A memory test which determines how accurately you can remember and recall information. There are two parts to this test and you will have a total of 10 minutes in which to answer 20 questions.

Now that you understand what the test involves, let's move onto some sample test questions.

CHAPTER 2
MECHANICAL COMPREHENSION TEST

During the Royal Air Force Airman/Airwoman test you will be required to sit a mechanical comprehension test. Mechanical comprehension tests are an assessment that measures an individual's ability to learn and understand mechanical concepts. The tests are usually multiple-choice in nature and present simple, frequently encountered mechanisms and situations. The majority of mechanical comprehension tests require a working knowledge of basic mechanical operations and the application of physical laws. On the following pages I have provided you with a number of example questions to help you prepare for the tests. Work through them as quickly as possible but remember to go back and check which ones you get wrong; more importantly, make sure you understand how the correct answer is reached.

In this particular exercise there are 20 questions and you have 10 minutes in which to answer them.

MECHANICAL COMPREHENSION TEST 1

You have 20 minutes to complete this test.

QUESTION 1

A block and tackle refers to a device which is used to:

    A. Place under the wheel of a car to stop it from rolling backward

    B. Catch large fish

    C. Leverage a stationary object

    D. Hoist an object upwards by means of rope and pulleys

Answer

QUESTION 2

Which man is carrying less weight?

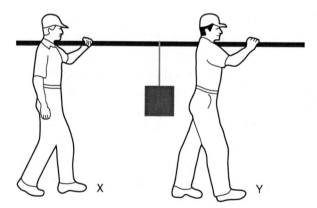

X   Y

    A. X

    B. Y

    C. Both the same

Answer

QUESTION 3

If wheel A rotates clockwise, which of the other wheels also rotate clockwise?

A.   All of them

B.   B, C, E, G and H

C.   D and F

D.   D, E and F

Answer [   ]

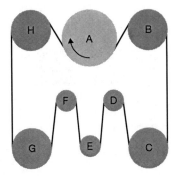

QUESTION 4

A builder is told to pitch his ladder a third of the working height away from the building below. How many metres away from the building should the foot of the ladder be placed?

A.   36 metres

B.   12 metres

C.   4 metres

D.   3 metres

Answer [   ]

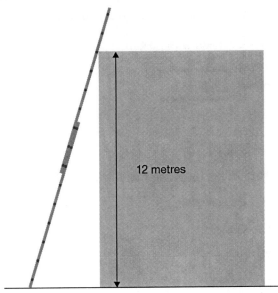

12 metres

QUESTION 5

What is the mechanical advantage in the diagram below?

A. 2

B. 4

C. 5

D. 6

Answer [   ]

QUESTION 6

A hot air balloon is able to float because:

A. The hot air is turbo-charged

B. The hot air is less dense than the external air

C. The hot air is denser than the external air

D. It is filled with helium

Answer [   ]

QUESTION 7

Which of the following materials will float on water?

A. Balsawood

B. Glass

C. Metal

D. Rock

Answer [   ]

QUESTION 8

Water is flowing into the following tank through the left-hand side inlet pipe at a rate of 18 litres per minute. If the water is flowing out through the lower right-hand side outlet pipe at a rate of 14 litres per minute, how much time will it take for the tank to overflow?

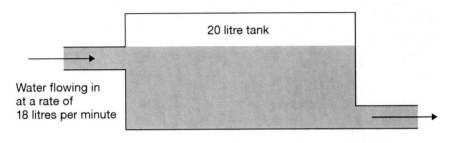

20 litre tank

Water flowing in
at a rate of
18 litres per minute

Water flowing out
at a rate of 14 litres per minute

A. 2 minutes

B. 3 minutes

C. 5 minutes

D. 8 minutes

Answer [ ]

QUESTION 9

How much weight will need to be placed on the right hand side to balance the beam?

A. 100 Kgs

B. 200 Kgs

C. 50 Kgs

D. 25 Kgs

Answer [ ]

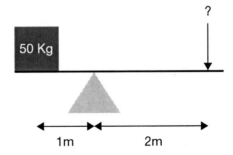

50 Kg   ?

1m   2m

QUESTION 10

If the wheel rotates anticlockwise, what will happen to X?

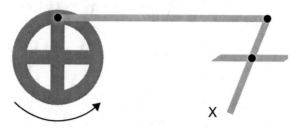

X

A. Move to the right and stop

B. Move to the left and stop

C. Move backwards and forwards

Answer

QUESTION 11

Which chain will support the load on its own?

A. A

B. B

C. C

D. None of them

Answer

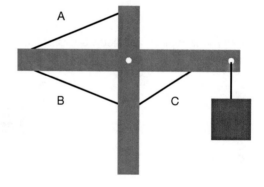

QUESTION 12

Which nail is likely to pull out first?

A. A

B. B

C. C

D. All of them at the same time

Answer [   ]

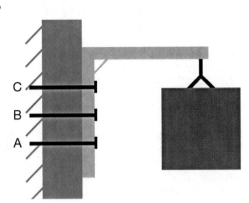

QUESTION 13

If wheel A rotates anticlockwise, which way and how will B rotate?

A. Clockwise faster

B. Clockwise slower

C. Anticlockwise faster

D. Anticlockwise slower

Answer [   ]

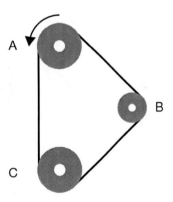

QUESTION 14

Which way and how will cog C rotate?

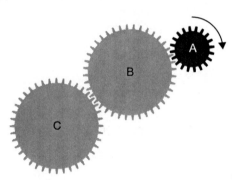

A.   Clockwise faster than A

B.   Clockwise slower than A

C.   Anticlockwise faster than A

D.   Anticlockwise slower A

Answer

QUESTION 15

Which lever will require more effort to lift the load?

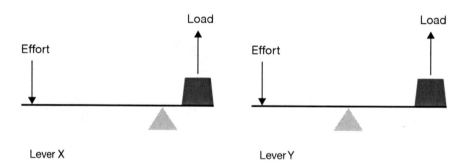

Lever X   Lever Y

A.   Lever X

B.   Lever Y

C.   Both the same

Answer

QUESTION 16

How much force is required to lift the load?

A.   140 Kgs

B.   210 Kgs

C.   90 Kgs

D.   70 Kgs

Answer [   ]

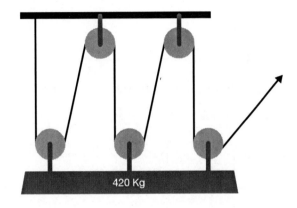

QUESTION 17

How much weight is required to hold the load?

A.   400 Kgs

B.   200 Kgs

C.   100 Kgs

D.   50 Kgs

Answer [   ]

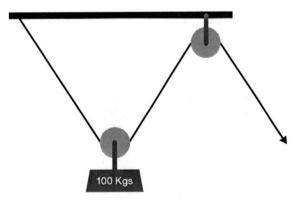

QUESTION 18

If lever A moves in the direction shown, which way will B move?

A. To the left

B. To the right

C. Backwards and forwards

D. It will not move

Answer

QUESTION 19

If the motor wheel rotates in a clockwise direction, then:

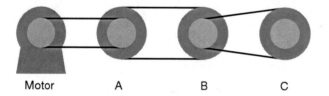

Motor   A   B   C

A. B and C move clockwise

B. B and C move anticlockwise

C. B moves clockwise and C moves anticlockwise

D. B moves anticlockwise, and C moves clockwise

Answer

QUESTION 20

If weight is placed on the top of each stack of boxes, which stack would support the most weight?

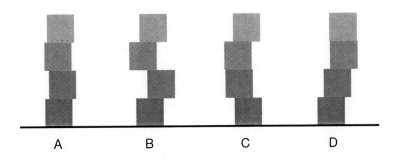

A   B   C   D

A. A

B. B

C. C

D. D

Answer

ANSWERS TO MECHANICAL COMPREHENSION TEST 1

1. D

A block and tackle is used to hoist an object upwards by means of rope and pulleys

2. X

You will see that the object is closer to man Y than man X. Therefore, man X is carrying less weight.

3. C

Wheel F and D are the only other wheels which will rotate clockwise.

4. C

The working height is 12 metres; therefore, the foot of the ladder must be placed 4 metres away from the building.

5. D

120kgs ÷ 20kgs = mechanical advantage of 6

6. B

The hot air inside a hot air balloon is less dense than the external air.

7. A

Balsawood is the only material here that will float on water.

8. C

Water is flowing in at a rate of 18 litres per minute; however, because water is also leaving the tank at a rate of 14 litres per minute, this means that only 4 litres per minute is effectively filling the tank. If the tank has a capacity of 20 litres then it will take 5 minutes for it to overflow.

9. D

In order to calculate the weight required in this type of situation you can make use of the following formula:

$$f = (w \times d1) \div d2$$

f = force required
w = weight
d1 = distance 1
d2 = distance 2

Answer: $f = (50 \times 1) \div 2$
(50 ÷ 2 is the same as 25 ÷ 1; the force required is 25 Kg)

10. C

It will move backwards and forwards as the wheel rotates.

11. B

Chain B is the only one which can support the load independently.

12. C

Nail C is most likely to pull out first.

13. C

Wheel B will rotate anticlockwise and faster because it is smaller than the other two wheels.

14. B

Cog C will rotate clockwise and slower than A because it has more teeth.

15. B

Lever Y will require more effort to lift the load because the fulcrum is further away from the load than level X.

16. D

The load weighs 420 Kgs and there are a total of six sections of rope supporting it. In order to calculate the force required to lift the load simply divide the weight by the number of ropes in order to reach your answer:

$420 \div 6 = 70$ Kgs

17. D

In this scenario the weight is suspended by two pulleys. This means the weight is split equally between the two pulleys. If you want to hold the weight you only have to apply half the weight of the load, i.e.

$100 \div 2 = 50$ Kgs.

18. A

B will move to the left in this situation.

19. A

B and C will move clockwise is the motor wheel moves clockwise.

20. A

Stack A is the most stable and will therefore support the most weight.

MECHANICAL COMPREHENSION TEST 2

You have 20 minutes to complete this test.

QUESTION 1

Which weight requires the most force to lift it?

A. Both the same

B. A

C. B

Answer

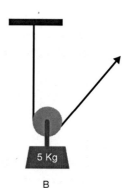

A   B

QUESTION 2

How much weight is required to balance point X?

A. 5Kg

B. 10Kg

C. 15Kg

D. 20Kg

Answer

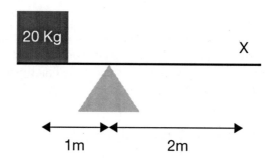

20 Kg   X

1m   2m

QUESTION 3

If cog C turns anti-clockwise at a speed of 10rpm, which way and at what speed will cog B turn?

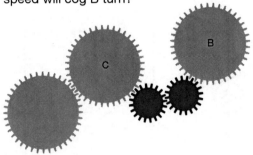

A. 10rpm / anti-clockwise

B. 10rpm / clockwise

C. 20rpm / anti-clockwise

D. 20rpm / clockwise

Answer

QUESTION 4

Which tool would you use to claw nails from wood?

A. 1

B. 2

C. 3

D. 4

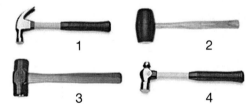

Answer

QUESTION 5

If bulb 2 is removed which bulbs will illuminate?

A.   1

B.   3

C.   4

D.   None

Answer [   ]

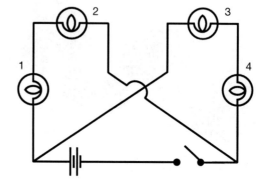

QUESTION 6

When the switch is closed how many bulbs will illuminate when bulb 3 is removed?

A.   None

B.   One

C.   Two

D.   Three

Answer [   ]

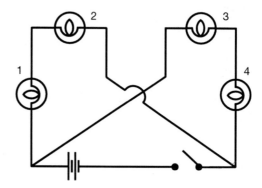

QUESTION 7

If cog B turns anti-clockwise which way will cog A turn?

A.   Clockwise

B.   Anti-clockwise

Answer

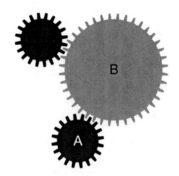

QUESTION 8

If wheel A is three times the diameter of wheel B and it rotates at 55rpm, what speed will wheel B rotate at?

A.   55 rpm

B.   110 rpm

C.   165 rpm

Answer

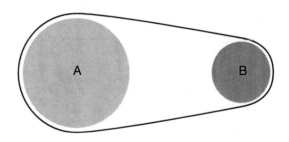

QUESTION 9

How much force is required to lift the 75 kg weight?

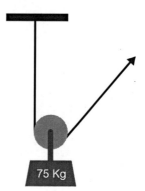

A.   15 kg

B.   37.5 kg

C.   75 kg

D.   150 kg

Answer [   ]

QUESTION 10

A screw has 8 threads per inch. How many full turns are required for the nut to travel 3 inches?

A.   8 turns

B.   12 turns

C.   16 turns

D.   24 turns

Answer [   ]

QUESTION 11

Cog A has 12 teeth and Cog B has 18 teeth. If cog B completes two full turns, how many rotations will cog A complete?

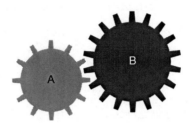

A.   3 rotations

B.   2 rotations

C.   1.5 rotations

D.   1 rotation

Answer [   ]

QUESTION 12

If cog 4 turns anti-clockwise, which other cogs will also turn anti-clockwise?

A.   Cog 1 only

B.   Cogs 1 and 3

C.   Cog 3 only

D.   Cogs 2 and 3

Answer [   ]

QUESTION 13

A thick block of wood rests on an even and level surface. What mechanical principle makes it more difficult to push this block sideways if the surface is made of sandpaper than if it is made of glass?

A. Spring force

B. Gravitational force

C. Air resistance force

D. Frictional force

Answer

QUESTION 14

When water is poured in to a tank, what happens to the pressure on the surface?

A. Decreases

B. Stays the same

C. Increases

Answer

QUESTION 15

The following three HGV's are parked on an incline. Their centre of gravity is identified by a dot. Which of the three HGV's is less most to fall over?

A. A

B. B

C. C

Answer [   ]

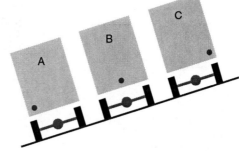

QUESTION 16

Which of the following most resembles a lever?

A. Swing

B. Car

C. Elevator

D. Seesaw

Answer [   ]

QUESTION 17

To balance the beam how much weight should be placed on the right hand side?

A. 5 kg

B. 10 kg

C. 15 kg

D. 30 kg

Answer [   ]

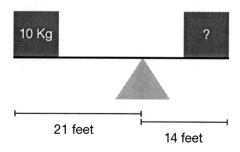

QUESTION 18

How far from the balance point should the 30 kg weight be placed to balance the beam?

A. 5 feet

B. 10 feet

C. 15 feet

D. 45 feet

Answer [   ]

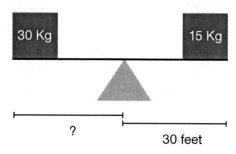

QUESTION 19

How far would you have to pull the rope up to lift the weight 5 feet?

A. 5 feet

B. 10 feet

C. 15 feet

D. 30 feet

Answer [   ]

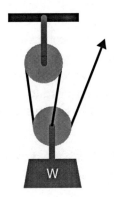

QUESTION 20

If cog X turns 40 times, how many times will cog Y turn?

A. 40 turns

B. 80 turns

C. 120 turns

D. 160 turns

Answer [   ]

ANSWERS TO MECHANICAL COMPREHENSION TEST 2

1. B

    When answering questions where there is a single pulley system if the pulley is fixed, as in A, then the force required to lift the weight is the same as the weight, i.e. 5Kg. However, where the pulley system is not fixed and it moves with the weight, as is the case with pulley system B, then the weight required to lift it is half the weight. This means that the weight required to lift B is 2.5kg. The answer to the questions is therefore B as pulley system A requires the most weight to lift it.

2. B

    Point X is twice the distance from the balance point; therefore, half the weight is required. The answer is B, 10Kg.

3. B

    If cog C turns 10 anti-clockwise at a speed of 10rpm then it is relatively straight forward to determine that cog B will rotate the same speed but in a clockwise direction.

4. A

    The only tool that you can use from the selection to claw nails from wood is claw hammer A.

5. D

    No bulbs would illuminate because the circuit, in its current state, is not working. This is due to the switch being open.

6. C

    Only two bulbs would illuminate (bulbs 1 and 2). The broken circuit would prevent bulb 4 from illuminating.

7. A

    Cog A will turn clockwise.

8. C

    Because wheel A is three times greater in diameter than wheel B, each revolution of A will lead to 3 times the revolution of B. Therefore, if wheel A rotates at 55 rpm, B will rotate at 55 rpm × 3 = 165 rpm.

9. B

This type of pulley system has a mechanical advantage of 2. Therefore, to lift the 75 kg weight will require 75kg ÷ 2 = 37.5 kg.

10. D

There are 8 threads per inch. To move the nut 3 inches will require 8 × 3 = 24 turns.

11. A

Each full turn of cog B will result in 18 teeth ÷ 12 teeth = 1.5 rotations. Two turns of cog B will result in cog A completing 3 rotations.

12. B

Cogs 1 and 3 will also turn anti-clockwise. Cog 2 is the only cog which will rotate clockwise.

13. D

In this particular case frictional force is the force that must be overcome in order to slide the object from one side to another.

14. B

The pressure at the surface remains the same, since it has a finite amount of water above it.

15. A

By drawing a vertical line straight down from the centre of gravity, only the line for HGV A reaches the ground outside of its tyres. This makes the HGV unstable.

16. D

A seesaw is the only option which utilises a form of leverage to function.

17. C

The distance of the weight on the right hand side from the balance point is one third less than the distance on the right hand side; therefore, an additional third weight is required to balance the beam.

18. C

In order to balance the beam the weight needs to be placed half the distance of the right hand side (15 feet). This is because the weight on the left is twice as heavy as the weight on the right hand side.

19. C

You would need to lift the rope 15 feet in order to lift the weight 5 feet.

20. D

Cog X has a total of 20 teeth, whereas cog Y has a total of 5 teeth. Because cog Y has four times fewer teeth than cog X, it will rotate four times for every single full rotation cog X achieves.

MECHANICAL COMPREHENSION TEST 3

You have 20 minutes to complete this test.

QUESTION 1

How many switches need to be closed in order to light up 3 bulbs?

A. 1

B. 2

C. 3

D. 4

Answer

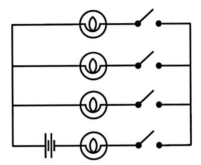

QUESTION 2

How many switches need to be closed in order to light up 1 bulb?

A. 1

B. 2

C. 3

D. 4

Answer

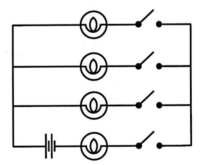

QUESTION 3

If bulb D is removed how which lights will remain illuminated?

A. Lights A, B and C

B. Lights A and B

C. Lights B and C

D. No lights

Answer

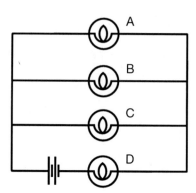

QUESTION 4

A ball is attached to a piece of string which in turn is secured to a ceiling. The ball and string are then held close to your nose but do not touch it. The ball and string are then released and allowed to swing away from you. When they swing back towards you, will they touch your face if you remain still?

A. Yes

B. No

Answer

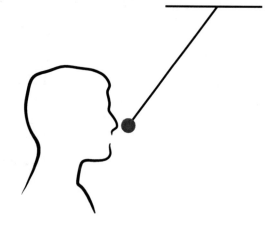

QUESTION 5

The glass on the left hand side contains water and oil. If you were to now add more water, what would the container look like?

  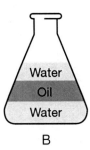 

A. Container A

B. Container B

C. Container C

Answer

QUESTION 6

Which spanner will it be harder to tighten the bolt with?

A.   Spanner A

B.   Spanner B

C.   Both the same

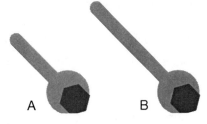

Answer

QUESTION 7

Which stick will be easier to balance?

A. Stick A

B. Stick B

C. Both the same

Answer

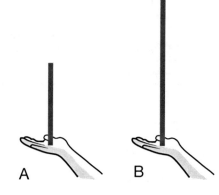

A   B

QUESTION 8

If wheel 2 is rotating clockwise, which other wheels will also rotate clockwise?

A. Wheels 1, 3, 4 and 5

B. Wheels, 1 and 5

C. Wheels 3 and 4

D. None of them

Answer

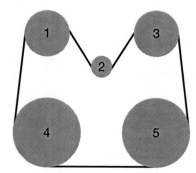

QUESTION 9

If wheel 4 is rotating anticlockwise, which other wheels will also rotate anticlockwise?

A. Wheels 1, 2, 3 and 5

B. Wheels, 1, 3 and 5

C. Wheels 2 and 5

D. None of them

Answer

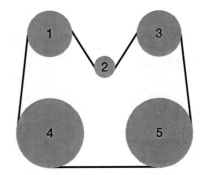

QUESTION 10

If cog B rotates anticlockwise by 10 rotations, how will cog A rotate?

A. Clockwise 5 rotations

B. Anticlockwise 20 rotations

C. Clockwise 20 rotations

D. Anticlockwise 5 rotations

Answer

QUESTION 11

How far from the fulcrum point would you place the 25 kgs weight in order to balance the bar?

A. 20 feet

B. 15 feet

C. 12 feet

D. 8 feet

Answer [   ]

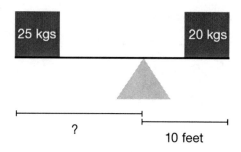

?

10 feet

QUESTION 12

If bar A moves to the left how will cog B rotate?

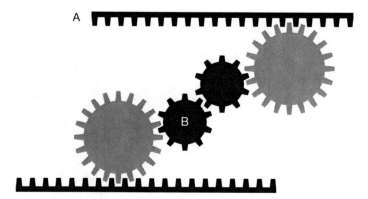

A. Clockwise

B. Anticlockwise

C. It won't move

Answer [   ]

QUESTION 13

In order to balance the bar below which way should the fulcrum be moved?

A.   Closer to ball X

B.   Closer to ball Y

Answer [   ]

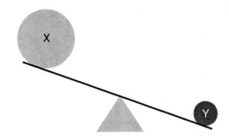

QUESTION 14

If the large piston has 4 times the surface area of the small piston, how far must the small piston be pushed down in order to raise the large piston 1 cm?

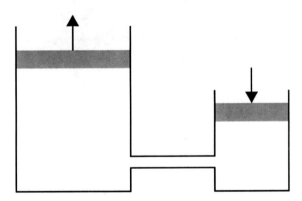

A.   0.5 cm

B.   1 cm

C.   2 cm

D.   4 cm

Answer [   ]

QUESTION 15

At what point is the velocity of a bullet fastest?

    A. When it leaves the muzzle

    B. When it reaches the top of its arc

    C. When it hits the target

Answer

QUESTION 16

If cog B makes 21 rotations, how many will cog A make?

    A. 21

    B. 14

    C. 7

    D. 30

Answer

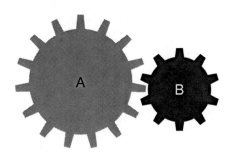

QUESTION 17

On which pole is there the most pressure?

    A. Pole 1

    B. Pole 2

    C. Both the same

Answer

 1

 2

QUESTION 18

Which term below describes the OPPOSITE of a decrease in speed?

A. Rotation

B. Acceleration

C. Friction

D. Velocity

Answer

QUESTION 19

A valve is used to perform which of the following tasks?

A. Control the flow of a liquid

B. Increase the temperature of a liquid

C. Facilitate the evaporation of a liquid

D. Decrease the density of a liquid

Answer

QUESTION 20

A lift is most similar to which of the following mechanical devices?

A. Spring

B. Hydraulic jet

C. Lever

D. Crane

Answer

ANSWERS TO MECHANICAL COMPREHENSION TEST 3

1. C

In order to illuminate 3 bulbs there needs to be at least 3 switches closed.

2. B

In order to illuminate 1 bulb there needs to be at least 2 switches closed.

3. D

If bulb D is removed then the circuit will be broke and no lights will illuminate.

4. B

They will not touch your face because there is insufficient speed or force for the ball to travel further than the point of origin.

5. C

Container C is the correct answer as water is denser than oil.

6. A

Spanner A will be harder to tighten the bolt with, simply because the smaller handle creates less leverage.

7. B

Stick B will be easier to balance because there is more weight at the palm of the hand.

8. D

The only wheel that is rotating clockwise is wheel 2.

9. B

Wheels 1, 3 and 5 will also rotate anti-clockwise, whereas wheel 2 will rotate clockwise.

10. C

Cog A will rotate clockwise 20 rotations. In order to work this out simply count the number of teeth on both cog A and cog B. You will see that cog A has 5 teeth, whereas cog B had 10 teeth. For every one full rotation of cog B, cog A will rotate two full turns.

11. D

The 25 kgs weight would need to be positioned 8 feet from the fulcrum point to balance the bar.

12. B

Cog B will rotate anticlockwise if bar A moves to the left.

13. B

The fulcrum must be moved closer to ball Y in order to balance the bar. We can assume that ball X is lighter than ball Y; therefore, we need to move the fulcrum closer to Y in order to balance the bar. Do not be fooled by ball X being larger than ball Y and assume that X is heavier. Ball Y is clearly heavier than ball X, despite being smaller in size.

14. D

Because the larger piston is 4 times the surface area the smaller piston will need to be pushed down 4 cm in order to move the large piston 1 cm.

15. A

The bullet will be fastest when it leaves the muzzle. Thereafter, the velocity will decrease.

16. B

Cog A has 15 teeth and cog B has 10 teeth. If cog B makes 21 rotations cog A will make one third fewer.

17. A

There will be more pressure on 1 as the majority of the weight is resting on it.

18. B

Acceleration is the opposite of deceleration.

19. A

A valve is used to control the flow of liquid.

20. D

A crane is similar to a lift in terms of mechanical function.

CHAPTER 3
VERBAL REASONING TEST

VERBAL REASONING TEST – EXERCISE 1

Read the following information carefully before answering the questions that follow. You have 5 minutes to complete exercise 1.

FLAT A is located in a town. It is 12 miles from the nearest train station. It has 2 bedrooms and is located on the ground floor. The monthly rental is £450 and the council tax is £50 per month. The lease is for 6 months.

FLAT B is located in the city centre and is 2 miles from the nearest train station. It is located on the 3rd floor. The monthly rental is £600 and the council tax is £130 per month. The lease is for 6 months and it has 3 bedrooms.

FLAT C is located in the city centre and is 3 miles from the nearest train station. It is located on the 1st floor and has 1 bedroom. The monthly rental is £550 and the council tax is £100 per month. The lease is for 12 months.

FLAT D is located in a town. The monthly rental is £395 per month and the council tax is £100 per month. It is located on the ground floor and the lease is for 6 months. It is 18 miles from the nearest train station. The flat has 2 bedrooms.

FLAT E is located in a village and is 12 miles from the nearest train station. It has 3 bedrooms and is located on the 2nd floor. The monthly rental is £375 and the council tax is £62.

QUESTION 1

You want a flat that is within 10 miles of the nearest train station and is located on the 1st floor or lower. The combined monthly rent/council tax bill must be no greater than £600. Which flat would you choose?

A. Flat A

B. Flat B

C. Flat C

D. Flat D

E. None of the above

Answer [   ]

QUESTION 2

You want a flat that has at least 2 bedrooms and has a combined monthly rent/council tax bill that does not exceed £450. Which flat would you choose?

A. Flat A

B. Flat B

C. Flat C

D. Flat D

E. Flat E

Answer [   ]

QUESTION 3

You want a flat that has a combined monthly rent/council tax bill that is not in excess of 700, is within 20 miles of the nearest train station and has a lease of at least 6 months. Which flat would you choose?

A. Flat A

B. Flat B

C. Flat C

D. Flat D

E. Flat E

Answer [   ]

VERBAL REASONING TEST – EXERCISE 2

Read the following information carefully before answering the questions that follow. You have 5 minutes to complete exercise 2.

Barry and Bill work at their local supermarket in the town of Whiteham. Barry works every day except Wednesdays. The supermarket is run by Barry's brother Elliot who is married to Sarah. Sarah and Elliot have 2 children called Marcus and Michelle who are both 7 years old and they live in the road adjacent to the supermarket. Barry lives in a town called Redford, which is 7 miles from Whiteham. Bill's girlfriend Maria works in a factory in her hometown of Brownhaven. The town of Redford is 4 miles from Whiteham and 6 miles from the seaside town of Tenford. Sarah and Elliot take their children on holiday to Tenford twice a year and Barry usually gives them a lift in his car. Barry's mum lives in Tenford and he tries to visit her once a week at 2pm when he is not working.

QUESTION 1

Which town does Elliot live in?

- **A.** Redford
- **B.** Whiteham
- **C.** Brownhaven
- **D.** Tenford
- **E.** Cannot say

Answer [   ]

QUESTION 2

On which day of the week does Barry visit his mother?

- **A.** Cannot say
- **B.** Monday
- **C.** Tuesday
- **D.** Wednesday
- **E.** Thursday

Answer [   ]

QUESTION 3

Bill and Maria live together in Brownhaven.

- **A.** True
- **B.** False
- **C.** Cannot say

Answer [   ]

VERBAL REASONING TEST – EXERCISE 3

Read the following information carefully before answering the questions that follow. You have 5 minutes to complete exercise 3.

Janet and Steve have been married for 27 years. They have a daughter called Jessica who is 25 years old. They all want to go on holiday together but cannot make up their minds where to go. Janet's first choice would be somewhere hot and sunny abroad. Her second choice would be somewhere in their home country that involves a sporting activity. She does not like hill climbing or walking holidays but her third choice would be a skiing holiday. Steve's first choice would be a walking holiday in the hills somewhere in their home country and his second choice would be a sunny holiday abroad. He does not enjoy skiing. Jessica's first choice would be a skiing holiday and her second choice would be a sunny holiday abroad. Jessica's third choice would be a walking holiday in the hills of their home country.

QUESTION 1

Which holiday are all the family most likely to go on together?

A. Skiing

B. Walking

C. Holiday Abroad

D. Sporting activity holiday

E. Cannot Say

Answer ⬚

QUESTION 2

If Steve and Jessica were to go on holiday together where would they be most likely to go?

A. Sunny holiday abroad

B. Skiing

C. Cannot say

D. Sporting activity holiday

E. Walking

Answer ⬚

QUESTION 3

Which holiday are Janet and Steve most likely to go on together?

A. Cannot say

B. Walking

C. Sporting activity holiday

D. Skiing

E. Sunny holiday abroad

Answer ⬚

VERBAL REASONING TEST – EXERCISE 4

Read the following information carefully before answering the questions that follow. You have 5 minutes to complete exercise 4.

Cardiovascular disease is so prevalent that virtually all businesses are likely to have employees who suffer from, or may develop, this condition. Research shows that between 51-80% of all people who suffer a heart attack are able to return to work. However, this may not be possible if they have previously been involved in heavy physical work. In such cases, it may be possible to move the employee to lighter duties, with appropriate retraining where necessary. Similarly, high-pressure, stressful work, even where it does not involve physical activity, should also be avoided. Human Resources managers should be aware of the implications of job roles for employees with a cardiac condition.

QUESTION 1

Physical or stressful work may bring on a heart attack?

   A. True

   B. False

   C. Cannot say based on the information provided.

Answer

QUESTION 2

The majority of people who have suffered a heart attack can later return to work.

   A. True

   B. False

   C. Cannot say based on the information provided.

Answer

QUESTION 3

Heart disease may affect employees in any type of business.

   A. True

   B. False

   C. Cannot say based on the information provided.

Answer

VERBAL REASONING TEST – EXERCISE 5

Read the following information carefully before answering the questions that follow. You have 5 minutes to complete exercise 4.

Abdominal pain in children may be a symptom of emotional disturbance, especially where it appears in conjunction with phobias or sleep disorders such as nightmares or sleep-walking. It may also be linked to eating habits: a study carried out in the USA found that children with pain tended to be fussier about what and how much they ate, and to have over-anxious parents who spent a considerable time trying to persuade them to eat. Although abdominal pain had previously been linked to excessive milk-drinking, this research found that children with pain drank rather less milk than those in the control group.

QUESTION 1

There is no clear cause for abdominal pain in children.

A. True

B. False

C. Cannot say based on the information provided.

Answer

QUESTION 2

Abdominal pain in children is caused by eating too much.

A. True

B. False

C. Cannot say based on the information provided.

Answer

QUESTION 3

Drinking milk may help to prevent abdominal pain in children.

A. True

B. False

C. Cannot say based on the information provided.

Answer

VERBAL REASONING TEST – EXERCISE 6

Read the following information carefully before answering the questions that follow. You have 5 minutes to complete exercise 4.

Jeff Bridges claims he has had his garden shed broken into. A crowbar was found in the garden and the door of the shed had been forced open using it. Mr Bridges claims that a lawn mower, a strimmer, a new spade and a garden fork have been stolen. He says that last week a group of young people graffitied the side wall of his house and he thinks they are to blame. The ringleader of the gang, Sam Smith has recently started a gardening company.

The latest reported facts are:

- Sam Smith had previous convictions for breaking and entering.

- Sam Smith has a variety of new gardening equipment for his company – including a spade the same as Mr Bridges.

- Mr Bridges spade was bought from popular high street shop B & P.

- Mr Bridges claims the items stolen were worth £400.

- Mr Bridges says Sam Smith has been harassing him.

- Sam Smith's dad fired Mr Bridges from his marketing company last month.

QUESTION 1

Mr Bridges had a grudge against Sam Smith.

   A. True

   B. False

   C. Cannot say based on the information provided.

Answer [   ]

QUESTION 2

The items stolen from Mr Bridges shed are worth more than £400.

   A. True

   B. False

   C. Cannot say based on the information provided.

Answer [   ]

QUESTION 3

Sam Smith may have stolen Mr Bridges spade.

   A. True

   B. False

   C. Cannot say based on the information provided.

Answer [   ]

ANSWERS TO VERBAL REASONING TESTS

EXERCISE 1

1. E

2. E

3. C

EXERCISE 2

1. B

2. D

3. C

EXERCISE 3

1. C

2. A

3. E

EXERCISE 4

1. C

2. A

3. A

EXERCISE 5

1. A

2. C

3. C

EXERCISE 6

1. C

2. C

3. A

CHAPTER 4
NUMERICAL REASONING TEST

During the Airman/Airwoman Selection Test you will be required to undertake a numerical reasoning test. This test is used to determine how accurately you can interpret numerical information such as charts, graphs and tables. The test will also assess your ability to use fractions, decimals and different formula. As you can imagine, the most effective way to prepare for this type of test is to carry out lots of sample numerical reasoning test questions, without the aid of a calculator.

During the actual numerical reasoning test with the RAF you will have a specific amount of time to answer each question. It is important that you do not spend too much time on one particular question. Remember that the clock is ticking. Have a go at the first numerical reasoning exercise that now follows and use a blank sheet of paper to work out your calculations. Remember to check your answers very carefully. It is important that you check any incorrect answers to see why you got them wrong.

You have 10 minutes in which to answer the 20 questions. Calculators are not permitted.

NUMERICAL REASONING TEST – EXERCISE 1

You are not permitted to use a calculator during this exercise.

You have 10 minutes in which to answer 20 multiple-choice questions

QUESTION 1

Your friends tell you their electricity bill has gone up from £40 per month to £47 per month. How much extra are they now paying per year?

A. £84

B. £85

C. £83

D. £86

E. £82

Answer [   ]

QUESTION 2

A woman earns a salary of £32,000 per year. How much would she earn in 15 years?

A. £280,000

B. £380,000

C. £480,000

D. £260,000

E. £460,000

Answer [   ]

QUESTION 3

If a woman walks for 6 hours at a pace of 4km/h, how much ground will she have covered after the 6 hours is over?

A. 20km

B. 21km

C. 22km

D. 23km

E. 24km

Answer [   ]

QUESTION 4

It takes Malcolm 45 minutes to walk 6 miles to work. At what pace does he walk?

A. 7 mph

B. 4 mph

C. 6 mph

D. 5 mph

E. 8 mph

Answer [   ]

QUESTION 5

Ellie spends 3 hours on the phone talking to her friend abroad. If the call costs 12 pence per 5 minutes, how much does the call cost in total?

A. £3.30

B. £4.32

C. £3.32

D. £4.44

E. £3.44

Answer [   ]

QUESTION 6

A woman spends £27 in a retail store. She has a discount voucher that reduces the total cost to £21.60. How much discount does the voucher give her?

A. 5%

B. 10%

C. 15%

D. 20%

E. 25%

Answer [   ]

QUESTION 7

A group of 7 men spend £21.70 on a round of drinks. How much does each of them pay if the bill is split evenly?

  A. £3.00

  B. £65.10

  C. £3.10

  D. £3.15

  E. £3.20

Answer

QUESTION 8

45,600 people attend a football match to watch Manchester United play Tottenham Hotspur. If there are 32,705 Manchester United supporters at the game, how many Tottenham Hotspur supporters are there?

  A. 12,985

  B. 13,985

  C. 12,890

  D. 12,895

  E. 14, 985

Answer

QUESTION 9

The police are called to attend a motorway accident involving a coach full of passengers. A total of 54 people are on board, 17 of whom are injured. How many are not injured?

A. 40

B. 39

C. 38

D. 37

E. 36

Answer

QUESTION 10

A car journey usually takes 6 hrs and 55 minutes, but on one occasion the car stops for a total of 47 minutes. How long does the journey take on this occasion?

A. 6 hrs 40 mins

B. 5 hrs 45 mins

C. 7 hrs 40 mins

D. 7 hrs 42 mins

E. 6 hrs 42 mins

Answer

QUESTION 11

There are 10 people in a team. Five of them weigh 70 kg each and the remaining 5 weigh 75 kg each. What is the average weight of the team?

A. 72.5 kg

B. 71.5 kg

C. 70.5 kg

D. 72 kg

E. 71 kg

Answer [   ]

QUESTION 12

A kitchen floor takes 80 tiles to cover. A man buys 10 boxes, each containing 6 tiles. How many more boxes does he need to complete the job?

A. 2 boxes

B. 4 boxes

C. 6 boxes

D. 8 boxes

E. 10 boxes

Answer [   ]

QUESTION 13

How much money does it cost to buy 12 packets of crisps at 47 pence each?

A. £6.45

B. £5.64

C. £6.54

D. £4.65

E. £5.46

Answer [ ]

QUESTION 14

A motorcyclist is travelling at 78 mph on a road where the speed limit is 50 mph. How much over the speed limit is he?

A. 20 mph

B. 22 mph

C. 26 mph

D. 28 mph

E. 30 mph

Answer [ ]

QUESTION 15

A removal firm loads 34 boxes onto a van. If there are 27 boxes still to be loaded, how many boxes are there in total?

A. 49

B. 50

C. 61

D. 52

E. 53

Answer ⬚

QUESTION 16

When paying a bill at the bank you give the cashier one £20 note, two £5 notes, four £1 coins, six 10p coins and two 2p coins. How much have you given him?

A. £34.64

B. £43.46

C. £34.46

D. £63.44

E. £36.46

Answer ⬚

QUESTION 17

If you pay £97.70 per month on your council tax bill, how much would you pay quarterly?

    A. £293.30

    B. £293.20

    C. £293.10

    D. £293.00

    E. £292.90

Answer [   ]

QUESTION 18

Four people eat a meal at a restaurant. The total bill comes to £44.80. How much do they need to pay each?

    A. £10.00

    B. £10.10

    C. £10.20

    D. £11.10

    E. £11.20

Answer [   ]

QUESTION 19

A worker is required to work for 8 hours a day. He is entitled to three 20-minute breaks and one 1-hour lunch break during that 8-hour period. If he works for 5 days per week, how many hours will he have worked after 4 weeks?

A. 12 hours

B. 14 hours

C. 120 hours

D. 140 hours

E. 150 hours

Answer [   ]

QUESTION 20

If there are 610 metres in a mile, how many metres are there in 4 miles?

A. 240

B. 2040

C. 2044

D. 2440

E. 244

Answer [   ]

ANSWERS TO NUMERICAL REASONING TEST – EXERCISE 1

1. a. £84
    In this question you need to first work out the difference in their electricity bill. Subtract £40 from £47 to be left with £7. Now you need to calculate how much extra they are paying per year. If there are 12 months in a year then you need to multiply £7 by 12 months to reach your answer of £84.

2. c. £480,000
    The lady earns £32,000 per year. To work out how much she earns in 15 years, you must multiply £32,000 by 15 years to reach your answer of £480,000.

3. e. 24km
    To work this answer out all you need to do is multiply the 6 hours by the 4 km/h to reach the total of 24 km. Remember that she is walking at a pace of 4 km per hour for a total of 6 hours.

4. e. 8mph
    Malcolm walks 6 miles in 45 minutes, which means he is walking two miles every 15 minutes. Therefore, he would walk 8 miles in 60 minutes (1 hour), so he is walking at 8 mph.

5. b. £4.32
    If the call costs 12 pence for every 5 minutes then all you need to do is calculate how many 5 minutes there are in the 3-hour telephone call. There are 60 minutes in every hour, so therefore there are 180 minutes in 3 hours. 180 minutes divided by 5 minutes will give you 36. To get your answer, just multiply 36 by 12 pence to reach your answer of £4.32

6. d. 20%
    This type of question can be tricky, especially when you don't have a calculator! The best way to work out the answer is to first of all work out how much 10% discount would give you off the total price. If £27 is the total price, then 10% would be a £2.70 discount. In monetary terms the woman has received £5.40 in discount. If 10% is a £2.70 discount then 20% is a £5.40 discount.

7. c. £3.10
    Divide £21.70 by 7 to reach your answer of £3.10.

8. d. 12,895
    Subtract 32,705 from 45,600 to reach your answer of 12,895.

9. d. 37
    Subtract 17 from 54 to reach your answer of 37.

10. d. 7 hrs 42 minutes
    Add the 47 minutes to the normal journey time of 6 hrs and 55
    minutes to reach your answer of 7 hrs and 42 minutes.

11. a. 72.5 kg
    To calculate the average weight, you need to first of all add each
    weight together. Therefore, (5 x 70) + (5 x 75) = 725 kg. To find the
    average weight you must now divide the 725 by 10, which will give
    you the answer 72.5 kg.

12. b. 4 boxes
    The man has 10 boxes, each of which contains 6 tiles. He therefore
    has a total of 60 tiles. He now needs a further 20 tiles to cover the
    total floor area. If there are 6 tiles in a box then he will need a further 4
    boxes (24 tiles).

13. b. £5.64
    Multiply 12 by 47 pence to reach your answer of £5.64.

14. d. 28 mph
    Subtract 50 mph from 78 mph to reach your answer of 28 mph.

15. c. 61
    Add 34 to 27 to reach your answer of 61 boxes.

16. a. £34.64
    Add all of the currency together to reach the answer of £34.64.

17. c. £293.10
    To reach the answer you must multiply £97.70 by 3. Remember, a
    quarter is every 3 months.

18. e. £11.2
    Divide £44.80 by 4 people to reach your answer of £11.20.

19. c. 120 hours

First of all you need to determine how many 'real' hours he works each day. Subtract the total sum of breaks from 8 hours to reach 6 hours per day. If he works 5 days per week then he is working a total of 30 hours per week. Multiply 30 hours by 4 weeks to reach your answer of 120 hours.

20. d. 2440 metres

Multiply 4 by 610 metres to reach your answer of 2440 metres.

NUMERICAL REASONING TEST – EXERCISE 2

You are not permitted to use a calculator during this exercise. You have 15 minutes in which to answer 25 multiple-choice questions

QUESTION 1

In a biscuit tin there are 28 biscuits. If you were to divide these equally between a family of 4, how many biscuits would each family member get?

A. 7

B. 4

C. 8

D. 3.5

E. 5

Answer

QUESTION 2

A plane can carry 180 passengers. There are 36 rows on the plane. How many passengers are there on each row?

A. 9

B. 6

C. 7

D. 8

E. 5

Answer

QUESTION 3

You have been driving for 2 hours 15 minutes at a constant speed of 48 mph. How far have you driven so far?

A. 180 miles

B. 108 miles

C. 104 miles

D. 140 miles

E. 144 miles

Answer [   ]

QUESTION 4

A sprinter runs 200 metres in 22 seconds. How long would it take him to run 2,000 metres if he continued to run at the same speed?

A. 3 minutes 40 seconds

B. 3 minutes 20 seconds

C. 4 minutes 20 seconds

D. 3 minutes 15 seconds

E. 4 minutes 15 seconds

Answer [   ]

QUESTION 5

Samantha is a carpenter. She makes 3 oak tables for a family. The first table top measures 0.75 x 2 metres, the second measures 1.5 x 3 metres and the third measures 1.0 x 3 metres. What is the average area of the table tops?

A. 5 m²

B. 4 m²

C. 3 m²

D. 2 m²

E. 2.5 m²

Answer [   ]

QUESTION 6

Five students buy a pizza each. Each pizza costs £5.20. The students are each given 10% discount. What is the total bill for the students?

A. £23.20

B. £23.40

C. £23.60

D. £24.40

E. £24.60

Answer [   ]

QUESTION 7

At a campsite there are 240 tents. During a flood, 2.5% of the tents are damaged. How many tents were damaged during the flood?

   A. 6

   B. 8

   C. 5

   D. 9

   E. 4

Answer ☐

QUESTION 8

In your savings account there is £13,000. You decide to withdraw 40% to buy a car. How much money do you withdraw?

   A. £520

   B. £5,200

   C. £7,200

   D. £8,000

   E. £8,200

Answer ☐

QUESTION 9

You own a Ford Fiesta which is currently worth £8000. Since you bought the car it has depreciated in value by 30% of its original value. How much was the original value of the vehicle?

A. £8,240

B. £11,400

C. £10,400

D. £12,400

E. £12,450

Answer [   ]

QUESTION 10

A ticket for a football match costs £12. If 12,000 people go to the game, how much in total will ticket sales make?

A. £14,400

B. £144,000

C. £288,000

D. £144,0000

E. £420,000

Answer [   ]

QUESTION 11

A solicitor charges £28 per hour for legal services. If you hired a solicitor for 12 hours, how much would you be charged?

   A. £326

   B. £336

   C. £374

   D. £436

   E. £442

Answer

QUESTION 12

At Uxbridge Grammar there are 200 students. 15 of the students get straight A's. What is this as a percentage?

   A. 7.5%

   B. 10%

   C. 15%

   D. 30%

   E. 45%

Answer

QUESTION 13

You find a missing wallet in the street. It contains a £10 note, two £5 notes, three £1 coins, a 50p coin and six 2p coins. How much is in the wallet?

A. £22.72

B. £22.62

C. £24.62

D. £23.56

E. £23.62

Answer

QUESTION 14

Your car does 35 miles to the gallon. The car takes 8 gallons of petrol full. If you were to drive 560 miles how much petrol would you need?

A. 12 gallons

B. 14 gallons

C. 16 gallons

D. 18 gallons

E. 24 gallons

Answer

QUESTION 15

Two farmers, Jack and Tom, both own adjoining fields. What is the total combined area of both Jack's and Tom's fields?

A.   160m²

B.   240m²

C.   800m²

D.   1600m²

E.   2400m²

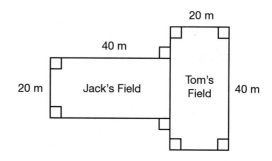

Answer [   ]

QUESTION 16

On average a bank repossesses 3 out of 150 homes every year. The village of Claxby has 1,000 homes. Under the above principle, how many homes would be repossessed in the village?

A.   10

B.   15

C.   20

D.   25

E.   30

Answer [   ]

QUESTION 17

A school has 15 classes with 23 students in each class. How many students are at the school?

A. 245

B. 325

C. 335

D. 445

E. 345

Answer ☐

QUESTION 18

A restaurant serves 60 customers a night. If on average each customer spends £30, what is the total average for the night?

A. £180

B. £1,600

C. £2,400

D. £1,800

E. £1,260

Answer ☐

QUESTION 19

A chocolate bar costs 59p. If you were to buy 6 chocolate bars, how much would it cost you?

A. £3.34

B. £3.45

C. £3.54

D. £4.24

E. £4.14

Answer _____

QUESTION 20

You fly a three-leg journey in a light aircraft. The total distance covered is 270 miles. What is the average distance of each leg?

A. 70 miles

B. 80 miles

C. 90 miles

D. 135 miles

E. 140 miles

Answer _____

QUESTION 21

A team of 12 explorers find the wreck of a ship. The ship contains 6 gold bars each worth £120,000. How much money does each team member make?

A.   £40,000

B.   £60,000

C.   £100,000

D.   £120,000

E.   £130,000

Answer ☐

QUESTION 22

Below is a pie-chart representing crime in the town of Upton. Based on an estimated 100 crimes, use the pie-chart below to estimate the number of burglary-related crimes.

A.   17

B.   20

C.   27

D.   34

E.   170

Answer ☐

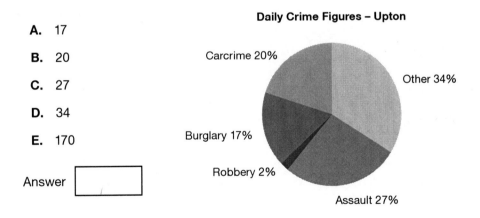

Daily Crime Figures – Upton

Carcrime 20%

Other 34%

Burglary 17%

Robbery 2%

Assault 27%

QUESTION 23

A magazine on average contains 110 pages. If you bought seven magazines, how many pages are there in total?

A. 700

B. 720

C. 740

D. 770

E. 780

Answer

QUESTION 24

A car is travelling at 72 miles per hour. How many miles will it have travelled in 45 minutes?

A. 54

B. 52

C. 50

D. 48

E. 46

Answer

QUESTION 25

If carpet costs 1.20 per metre, how much will 35 metres of carpet cost?

A. £45.00

B. £43.75

C. £44.00

D. £46.75

E. £42.00

Answer [   ]

ANSWERS TO NUMERICAL REASONING TEST – EXERCISE 2

1. A
2. E
3. B
4. A
5. C
6. B
7. A
8. B
9. C
10. B
11. B
12. A
13. E
14. C
15. D
16. C
17. E
18. D
19. C
20. C
21. B
22. A
23. D
24. A
25. E

CHAPTER 5
WORK RATE TEST

During the AST you will be required to undertake a work rate test. This form of test assesses your ability to work quickly and accurately whilst carrying out routine tasks; something which is integral to the role of an Airman/ Airwoman.

Before we move on to the test questions, let's take a look at a sample question. To begin with, study the following box which contains different numbers, letters and symbols.

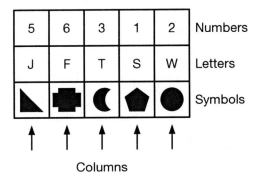

In the sample questions that I have provided you with, you will be given a code consisting of numbers, letters or symbols. Your task is to look at the 5 provided alternative codes and decide which one has been taken from the SAME columns as the original code.

For example, take a look at the following code:

CODE A – 563

Now look at the 5 alternatives, which are taken from the above grid and decide which code has been taken from the same columns as code A.

A.   **B.**   **C.**   **D.**   **E.**

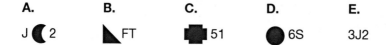

J ☾ 2   ◣ FT   ▦ 51   ⬤ 6S   3J2

You can see that the answer is in fact B and the code ◣ FT. The reason for this is that the code has been taken from the **same columns** as the original code of **563**.

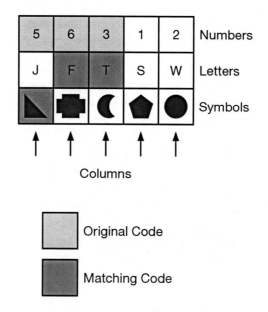

Now take the time to work through the following exercise. You have 10 minutes in which to work through the 10 questions.

WORK RATE TEST – EXERCISE 1

QUESTION 1

Which of the answers below is an alternative to the code **S87**?

8	7	1	2
■	◆	●	◣
S	E	T	H

A.   **B.**   **C.**   **D.**

8 ■ E   HS ●   ◣ S ◆   T ■ H

Answer [   ]

QUESTION 2

Which of the answers below is an alternative to the code **492**?

4	2	9	3
◆	■	◣	●
D	A	Q	X

A.   **B.**   **C.**   **D.**

D ◣ X   ◆ QA   ◣ AD   DAX

Answer [   ]

QUESTION 3

Which of the answers below is an alternative to the code **7Q1**?

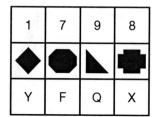

1	7	9	8
Y	F	Q	X

A.   **B.**   **C.**   **D.**

F ◣ Y   ◆ XY   ✚ Y ◆   QX ⬯

Answer [   ]

QUESTION 4

Which of the answers below is an alternative to the code **553**?

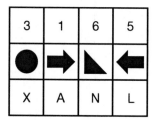

3	1	6	5
X	A	N	L

A.   **B.**   **C.**   **D.**

A ◣ X   ◣ AN   ➡ XL   ➡ LX

Answer [   ]

QUESTION 5

Which of the answers below is an alternative to the code **3QE**?

Q	D	W	E
P	➡	◣	7
1	3	Z	R

A.   **B.**   **C.**   **D.**

PZE   ◣ 17   ➡ 1R   Q3R

Answer [   ]

QUESTION 6

Which of the answers below is an alternative to the code **ADE**?

A	Q	R	E
1	⬅	✛	6
⬑	D	7	⬏

A.   **B.**   **C.**   **D.**

Q17   ⬑ Q6   ⬅ 16   ERA

Answer [   ]

QUESTION 7

Which of the answers below is an alternative to the code **6L4**?

L	1	R	■
2	●	✦	6
←	4	3	⬈

A.   **B.**   **C.**   **D.**

RL ⬈   ⬈ 21   ✦ L4   R62

Answer [   ]

QUESTION 8

Which of the answers below is an alternative to the code **L9R**?

L	1	R	£
2	9	&	6
=	4	3	>

A.   **B.**   **C.**   **D.**

61>   >9=   >1R   =13

Answer [   ]

QUESTION 9

Which of the answers below is an alternative to the code **1%Q**?

←	1	◣	%
1	●	&	⬏
Q	t	3	✚

A.

1&⬏

B.

13&

C.

t ✚ 1

D.

11&

Answer [   ]

QUESTION 10

Which of the answers below is an alternative to the code **>16**?

◆	6	⬅	%
1	●	+	◣
d	<	>	✚

A.

+d<

B.

d+<

C.

✚ d<

D.

1>%

Answer [   ]

ANSWERS TO WORK RATE TEST EXERCISE 1

1. A

2. B

3. A

4. D

5. C

6. B

7. B

8. D

9. C

10. A

Now move on to exercise 2. You have 12 minutes in which to work through the 15 questions.

WORK RATE TEST – EXERCISE 2

QUESTION 1

Which of the answers below is an alternative to the code **765**?

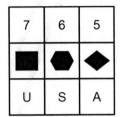

A.	B.	C.	D.
U 5	U ⬡ S	◆ 6U	US ◆

Answer [   ]

QUESTION 2

Which of the answers below is an alternative to the code **A8 ♥** ?

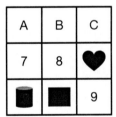

A.	B.	C.	D.
▮ C9	78 ▮	7B9	897

Answer [   ]

QUESTION 3

Which of the answers below is an alternative to the code **YEF**?

F	Y	E	W
▲	▶	▼	◀
2	4	8	1

A. 4 ▼ 1

B. ▶ 84

C. 481

D. ▶▼ 2

Answer [   ]

QUESTION 4

Which of the answers below is an alternative to the code **178**?

A	B	C	Z
7	8	3	1
▼	▶	◀	▲

A. ▲ A3

B. Z ▼ 3

C. ▲ AB

D. ▶ 3Z

Answer [   ]

QUESTION 5

Which of the answers below is an alternative to the code **82T**?

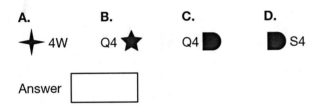

A.

✛ 4W

B.

Q4 ★

C.

Q4 ◗

D.

◗ S4

Answer [   ]

QUESTION 6

Which of the answers below is an alternative to the code **X39**?

D	S	E	X
9	3	2	5
0	1	4	8

A.

514

B.

8S2

C.

0S8

D.

51D

Answer [   ]

QUESTION 7

Which of the answers below is an alternative to the code **XWQ**?

■	●	▲	○
S	7	3	8
Q	X	W	K

A.　73 ●

B.　37K

C.　○ SX

D.　● 3 ■

Answer [　　　　]

QUESTION 8

Which of the answers below is an alternative to the code **482**?

I	B	N	M
8	7	4	2
▲	●	○	■

A.　NIM

B.　NBI

C.　7 ○ 2

D.　● MN

Answer [　　　　]

QUESTION 9

Which of the answers below is an alternative to the code **0W9**?

4	0	2	9
S	7	3	8
Q	X	W	K

A.   **B.**   **C.**   **D.**

X3Q   7X8   QS4   X28

Answer [   ]

QUESTION 10

Which of the answers below is an alternative to the code **672**?

U	Z	R	E
8	7	4	2
6	3	5	1

A.   **B.**   **C.**   **D.**

U31   6Z4   8Z5   3E8

Answer [   ]

QUESTION 11

Which of the answers below is an alternative to the code **3PJ**?

R	A	F	P
1	2	3	4
J	■	D	●

A. | **B.** | **C.** | **D.**

D ● A | 14F | ■ R3 | D41

Answer [   ]

QUESTION 12

Which of the answers below is an alternative to the code **72S**?

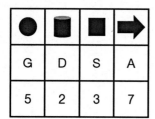

●	(cylinder)	■	➡
G	D	S	A
5	2	3	7

A. | **B.** | **C.** | **D.**

SD ➡ | AD3 | 52 ■ | A3D

Answer [   ]

QUESTION 13

Which of the answers below is an alternative to the code **1LS**?

R	A	F	P
J	S	2	4
●	H	■	L
1	▮	3	➡

A.	**B.**	**C.**	**D.**
RPF	P4 ➡	● 4 ▮	RAF

Answer [   ]

QUESTION 14

Which of the answers below is an alternative to the code **X1W3D**?

G	D	S	A	W	L
5	2	3	7	0	1
X	Y	Z	Q	E	T

A.	**B.**	**C.**	**D.**
51WZX	Y1QZT	GTEZY	YZ7SD

Answer [   ]

QUESTION 15

Which of the answers below is an alternative to the code **J4F**?

R		F	P
J			4
	H		L
1		3	

A.
1HF

B.
RPL

C.
31P

D.
1L3

Answer _____

ANSWERS TO WORK RATE TEST 2

1. D
2. C
3. D
4. C
5. C
6. D
7. D
8. A
9. D
10. A
11. D
12. B
13. C
14. C
15. D

CHAPTER 6
SPATIAL REASONING TEST

During the Airman/Airwoman Selection Test you will be required to undertake a spatial reasoning test.

The definition of spatial reasoning is as follows:

'The ability to interpret and make drawings from mental images and visualise movement or change in those images.'

During the AST you will be confronted with a number of spatial reasoning questions and the only effective way to prepare for them is to try as many as you can in the build up to the actual test. Let's now take a look at a sample question.

SAMPLE QUESTION

Take a look at the following 3 shapes. Note the letters on the side of each shape:

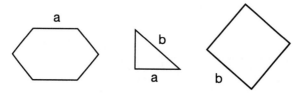

Join all of the 3 shapes together with the corresponding letters to make the following shape:

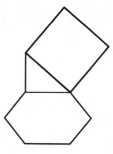

During the spatial reasoning exercise that now follows your task is to look at the given shapes and decide which of the examples matches the shape when joined together by the corresponding letters. You have 3 minutes to answer the 8 questions.

SPATIAL REASONING TEST 1

QUESTION 1

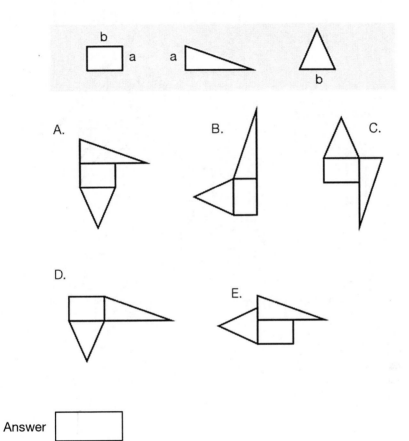

Answer [   ]

QUESTION 2

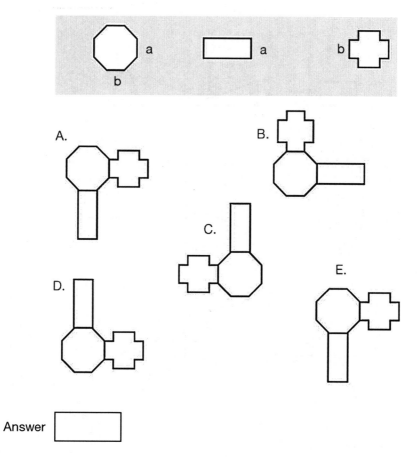

Answer [   ]

QUESTION 3

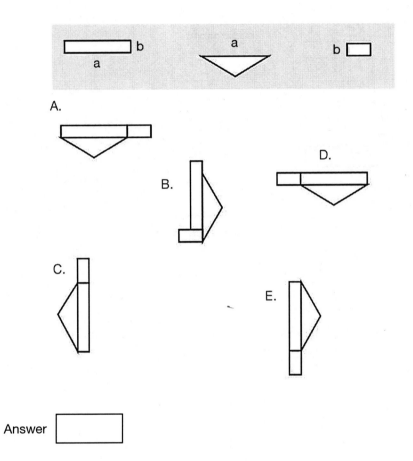

A.

D.

B.

C.

E.

Answer

QUESTION 4

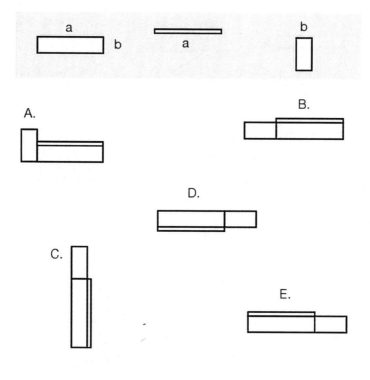

Answer [   ]

QUESTION 5

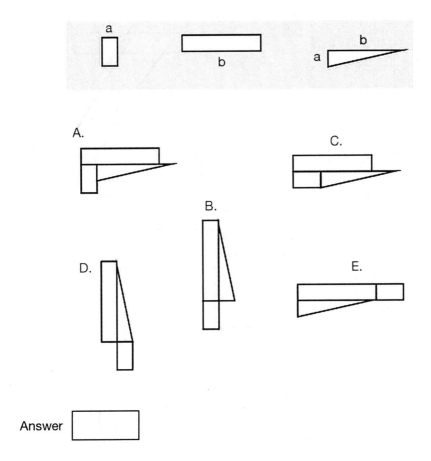

Answer [   ]

QUESTION 6

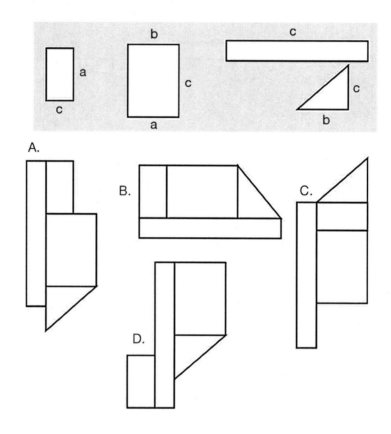

Answer [   ]

QUESTION 7

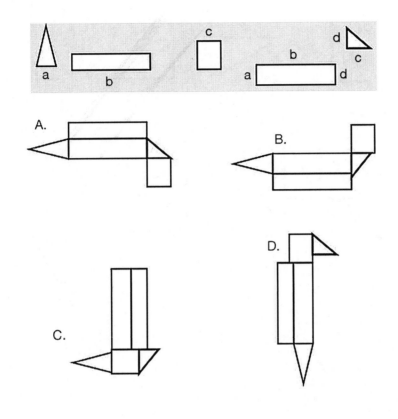

Answer [   ]

QUESTION 8

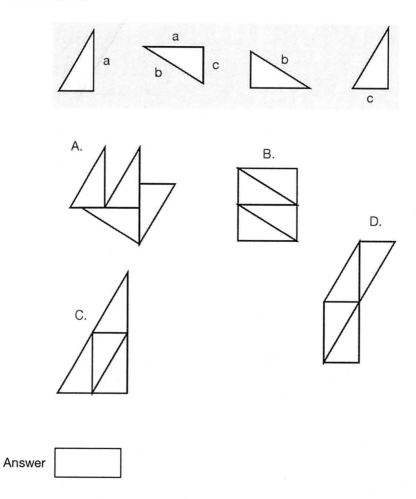

Answer [   ]

Now that you have completed the exercise take the time to work through your answers carefully. If you got any incorrect, make sure you understand how the correct answer is reached as this will assist you during your development.

ANSWERS TO SPATIAL REASONING TEST 1

1. B

2. D

3. A

4. E

5. D

6. B

7. A

8. C

SPATIAL REASONING TEST – EXERCISE 2

During the second spatial reasoning test that I've produced, you will be required to look at 3-dimensional objects. You have to imagine the 3-dimensional objects rotated in a specific way and then match them up against a choice of examples.

Look at the 2 objects below:

You now have to decide which of the 4 options provided demonstrates both objects rotated with the dot in the correct position. Look at the options below:

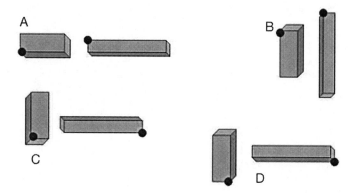

The correct answer is C

Now move on to spatial reasoning test exercise 2. You have 3 minutes in which to complete the 8 questions.

SPATIAL REASONING TEST EXERCISE 2

QUESTION 1

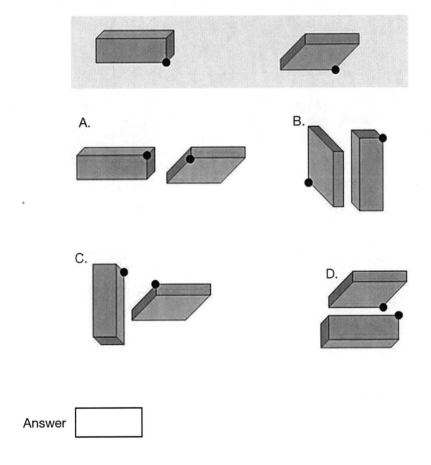

Answer [   ]

QUESTION 2

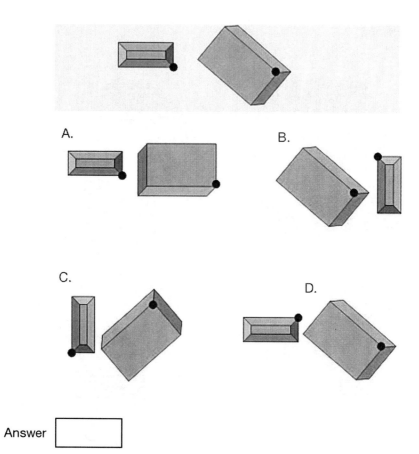

A.

B.

C.

D.

Answer

QUESTION 3

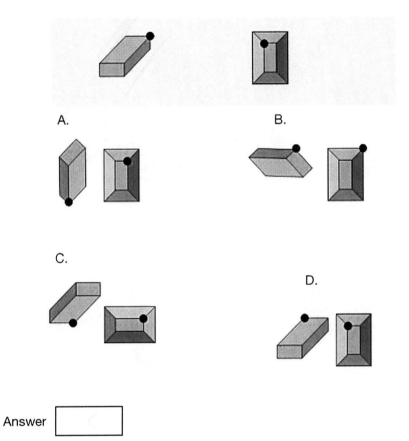

A.

B.

C.

D.

Answer _____

QUESTION 4

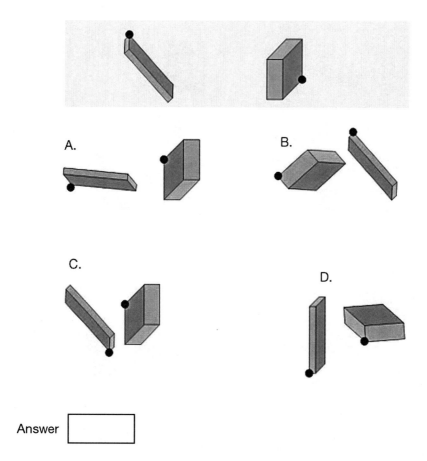

Answer [   ]

QUESTION 5

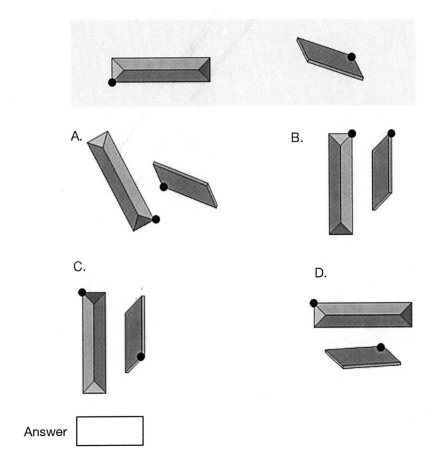

Answer ☐

QUESTION 6

A.

B.

C.

D.

Answer [   ]

QUESTION 7

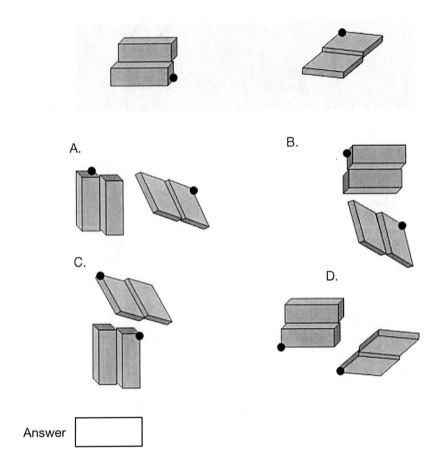

A.

B.

C.

D.

Answer [   ]

QUESTION 8

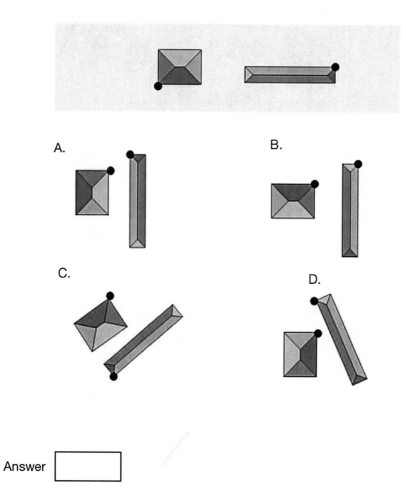

A.

B.

C.

D.

Answer [   ]

ANSWERS TO SPATIAL REASONING TEST EXERCISE 2

1. B

2. C

3. C

4. C

5. A

6. B

7. B

8. C

CHAPTER 7
ELECTRICAL COMPREHENSION TEST

During the AST you will be required to sit an Electrical Comprehension Test. The test itself is designed to assess your ability to work with different electrical concepts. On the following pages I have provided you with a number of sample questions to help you prepare for this test. Work through the questions as quickly as possible but remember to go back and check any questions that you may have got wrong. If you struggle to understand the concepts of electrical circuits and terminology then you may wish to purchase a booklet which will help you to understand how they work. You will be able to obtain a book from all good bookstores including www. amazon.co.uk.

In this particular exercise you have 10 minutes in which to answer the 20 questions.

ELECTRICAL COMPREHENSION TEST – EXERCISE 1

QUESTION 1

In the following circuit, how many switches need to close to light up 2 bulbs?

A.   0

B.   1

C.   2

D.   3

E.   4

Answer

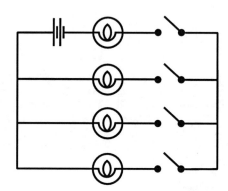

QUESTION 2

In the following circuit, how many switches need to close to light up 4 bulbs?

A.   0

B.   1

C.   2

D.   3

E.   4

Answer

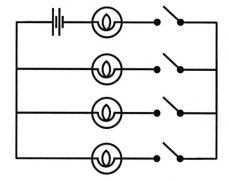

QUESTION 3

Identify the following electrical symbol:

 A. Fuse

 B. Switch

 C. Amplifier

 D. Voltmeter

 E. Variable resistor

Answer [   ]

QUESTION 4

Identify the following electrical symbol:

 A. Capacitor

 B. Ohmmeter

 C. Fuse

 D. Bulb

 E. Earphone

Answer [   ]

QUESTION 5

In the following circuit, if bulb 3 is removed and the switch is closed, which bulbs will illuminate?

A. No bulbs will illuminate

B. Bulb 4 only

C. Bulbs 1, 2 and 4

D. Bulbs 1 and 2

E. Bulbs 2 and 4

Answer

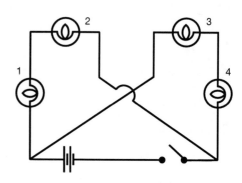

QUESTION 6

Which of the following is the symbol for a battery?

A. A

B. B

C. C

D. G

E. H

Answer

A

B   C

D   E   F

G   H   I

QUESTION 7

Which of the following is the symbol for a lamp?

A. D

B. E

C. F

D. G

E. None of these

Answer [　　　　　]

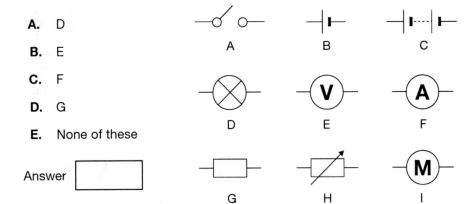

QUESTION 8

In the following circuit, if switches A and C close and bulb B is removed, which bulbs will illuminate?

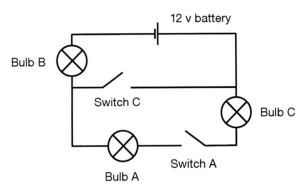

A. Bulb A only

B. Bulb B only

C. Bulbs A and B

D. No bulbs will illuminate

Answer [　　　　　]

QUESTION 9

Which of the following is the symbol for a variable resistor?

A. A

B. B

C. C

D. D

E. E

F. G

G. H

A

B

C

D

E

F

G

H

I

Answer [   ]

QUESTION 10

In the following circuit, how many bulbs will illuminate if switches 1, 2 and 4 close?

A. 2

B. 3

C. 4

D. 5

E. No bulbs will illuminate

Answer [   ]

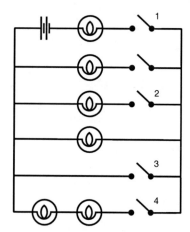

QUESTION 11

In the following circuit, how many bulbs will illuminate if switches 1 and 4 close?

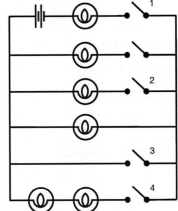

A.   2

B.   3

C.   4

D.   5

E.   No bulbs will illuminate

Answer [   ]

QUESTION 12

In the following circuit, if switch A closes and switch B remains open, what will happen?

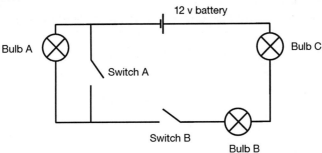

A.   No bulbs will illuminate

B.   Bulbs A, B and C will illuminate

C.   Bulb A will illuminate only

D.   Bulbs B and C will illuminate only

Answer [   ]

QUESTION 13

Insert the two missing words:

Voltage is a measure of the difference in _____ _____ between two parts of a circuit. The bigger the difference in energy, the bigger the voltage.

A. electrical energy

B. electrical current

C. flowing amperes

D. concurrent electricity

Answer [   ]

QUESTION 14

Insert the two missing words:

Current is a measure of how much _____ _____ flows through a circuit. The more charge that flows, the bigger the current.

A. electrical energy

B. electrical current

C. flowing amperes

D. electric charge

Answer [   ]

QUESTION 15

Which of the following substances is the worst electrical conductor?

A. Water

B. Rubber

C. Copper

D. Air

Answer

QUESTION 16

Ammeters measure the amount of current in a circuit. In the circuit below all the ammeters are identical. If Ammeter A1 reads 0.6A, what will Ammeter A3 read?

A. 0.12

B. 12.0

C. 0.4

D. 0.3

E. 3.0

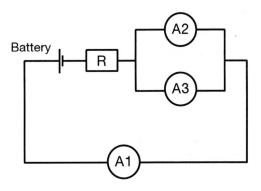

Answer

QUESTION 17

In the following electrical circuit, what will happen if the switch is open?

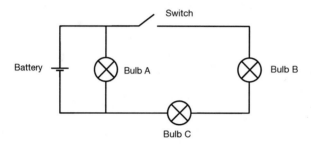

A. Bulbs A, B, C will illuminate

B. Bulbs A and B will illuminate only

C. Bulb A will illuminate only

D. No bulbs will illuminate

Answer

QUESTION 18

AC/DC – What do these abbreviations stand for?

A. Alternating Current, Direct Current

B. Analogue Current, Digital Current

C. Alternating Circuit, Direct Circuit

D. Analogue Circuit, Direct Circuit

Answer

QUESTION 19

What does a transformer do to electrical current?

A. Change its voltage

B. It turns electricity into power

C. It adds more watts

Answer [ ]

QUESTION 20

In a circuit diagram, what does a circle with a cross inside it represent?

A. A light bulb

B. A motor

C. A battery

D. A transformer

Answer [ ]

ANSWERS TO ELECTRICAL COMPREHENSION EXERCISE

1. C
2. E
3. C
4. C
5. D
6. C
7. A
8. D
9. G
10. D
11. C
12. A
13. A
14. D
15. B
16. D
17. C
18. A
19. A
20. A

CHAPTER 8
MEMORY TEST

During the Airman/Airwoman selection test you will be required to undertake a memory test. The test is usually in two parts. During the first part of the test you will be required to view a sequence of letters. The letters will appear on a screen for a period of time. After a period of time the sequence will disappear and you will then be required to answer questions relating to that sequence.

Let's assume that the sequence of letters looks like the following. Please note that during the real test the letters may appear individually over a set period of time and not collectively as per indicated below.

W	E	Q	X	R	E

Study the above sequence of letters for one minute only. Once the minute is up, cover the above sequence with your hand or a sheet of paper, and answer the following questions:

QUESTION 1

How many letter E's were there in the sequence?

Answer

QUESTION 2

How many letters were there in between the letter W and the letter X?

Answer [   ]

QUESTION 3

What letter was between the letter Q and the letter R?

Answer [   ]

Hopefully you managed to get the questions correct. Your ability to successfully pass this test will be dependant on how good your memory is.

ANSWERS TO SAMPLE TEST QUESTIONS

Question 1 – Two

Question 2 – Two

Question 3 – Letter X

In order to improve your ability during this test try the following sample exercise.

MEMORY TEST – EXERCISE 1

D	d	D	F	F	Q

Study the above sequence of letters for one minute only. Once the minute is up, cover the above sequence with your hand or a sheet of paper, and answer the following questions:

QUESTION 1

How many letter O's were in the sequence?

Answer _____

QUESTION 2

How many letter D's (both upper and lower case) were there in the sequence?

Answer _____

QUESTION 3

What was the last letter in the sequence?

Answer _____

MEMORY TEST – EXERCISE 2

A	a	T	M	N	Y

Study the above sequence of letters for one minute only. Once the minute is up, cover the above sequence with your hand or a sheet of paper, and answer the following questions:

QUESTION 1

How many letters were there in the entire sequence?

Answer ☐

QUESTION 2

How many lower case letters were there?

Answer ☐

QUESTION 3

What was the fourth letter in the sequence?

Answer ☐

MEMORY TEST – EXERCISE 3

G	H	W	K	B	U	Z

Study the above sequence of letters for one minute only. Once the minute is up, cover the above sequence with your hand or a sheet of paper, and answer the following questions:

QUESTION 1

How many letters were there in the entire sequence?

Answer [   ]

QUESTION 2

How many vowels were there in the sequence?

Answer [   ]

QUESTION 3

How many letters were there in between the letter G and the letter Z?

Answer [   ]

RAF AIRMAN TEST

MEMORY TEST – EXERCISE 4

s	a	A	q	a	W	A

Study the above sequence of letters for one minute only. Once the minute is up, cover the above sequence with your hand or a sheet of paper, and answer the following questions:

QUESTION 1

How many capital letters were there in the sequence?

Answer

QUESTION 2

How many lower case (non capital) letters were there in the sequence?

Answer

QUESTION 3

How many letter q's were there in the sequence?

Answer

MEMORY TEST – EXERCISE 5

C	E	A	r	Y	X	C	q

Study the above sequence of letters for one minute only. Once the minute is up, cover the above sequence with your hand or a sheet of paper, and answer the following questions:

QUESTION 1

What was the 6th letter in the sequence?

Answer

QUESTION 2

How many letters were there in the entire sequence?

Answer

QUESTION 3

How many vowels were there in the entire sequence?

Answer

ANSWERS TO MEMORY TEST EXERCISES

MEMORY TEST EXERCISE 1

1. 0

2. 3

3. Q

MEMORY TEST EXERCISE 2

1. 6

2. 1

3. M

MEMORY TEST EXERCISE 3

1. 7

2. 1

3. 5

MEMORY TEST EXERCISE 4

1. 3

2. 4

3. 1

MEMORY TEST EXERCISE 5

1. X

2. 8

3. 2

MEMORY TEST PART 2

During the second part of the test you will be required to view a number of different grids which contain coloured squares. Each grid will appear individually. Once the sequence of grids has disappeared you will be required to state which pattern the collective coloured squares make up from a number of different options.

Take a look at the following four grids. Please note: during the real test each grid will only appear one at a time and for a brief period. You will need to memorise the position of the coloured squares in each grid in order to answer the question.

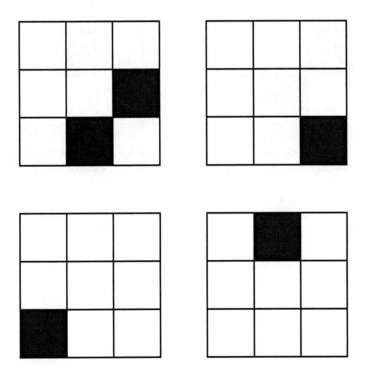

Once you have studied the grids cover them with your hand or a sheet of paper. Now decide from the following four options which grid contains the collective group of coloured squares from the four grids.

Option 1   Option 2

Option 3   Option 4

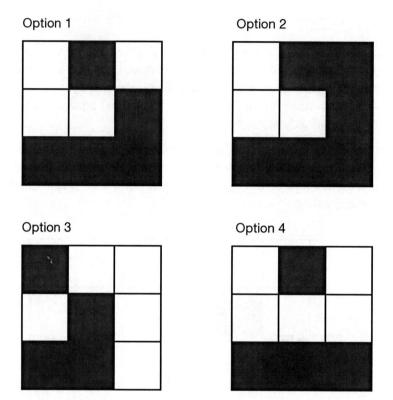

As you will see, **Option 1** accurately reflects the combined locations of the coloured squares from the initial four grids.

Once you understand what is required, move on to the following exercises.

MEMORY TEST PART 2 – EXERCISE 1

QUESTION 1

Study the following grids for 10 seconds only. Then turn the page and decide from the four options available which grid contains the collective group of coloured squares from the grids.

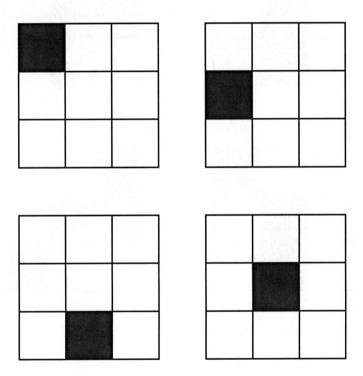

QUESTION 1 OPTIONS

A

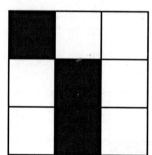

B

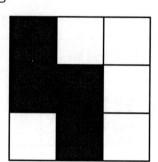

C

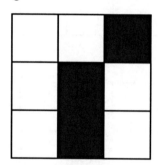

D

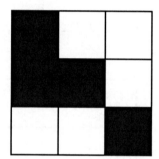

Answer [ ]

QUESTION 2

Study the following grids for 10 seconds only. Then turn the page and decide from the four options available which grid contains the collective group of coloured squares from the grids.

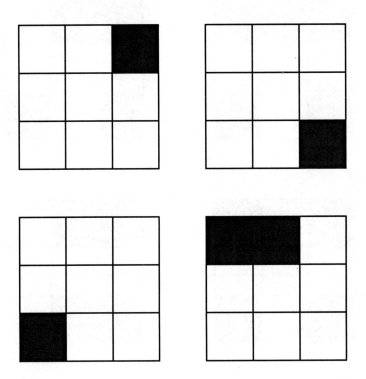

QUESTION 2 OPTIONS

A

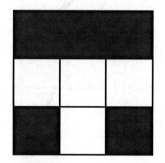

B

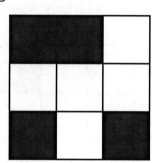

C

D

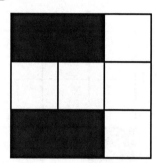

Answer [   ]

QUESTION 3

Study the following grids for 10 seconds only. Then turn the page and decide from the four options available which grid contains the collective group of coloured squares from the grids.

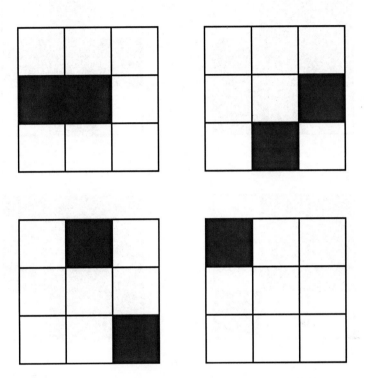

QUESTION 3 OPTIONS

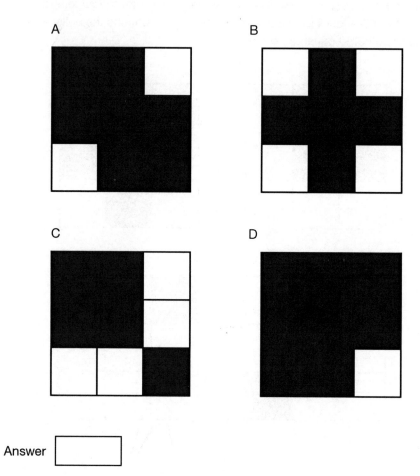

A

B

C

D

Answer

QUESTION 4

Study the following grids for 10 seconds only. Then turn the page and decide from the four options available which grid contains the collective group of coloured squares from the grids.

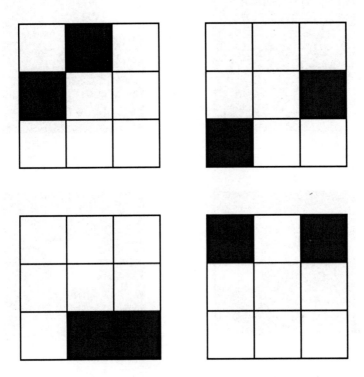

QUESTION 4 OPTIONS

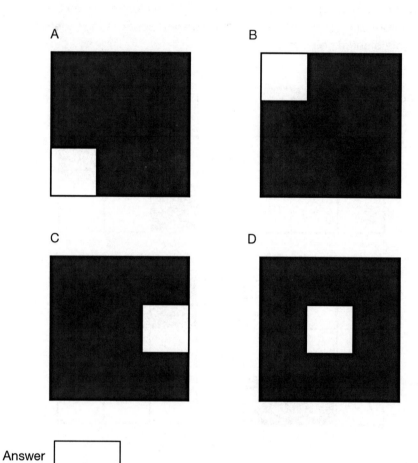

A

B

C

D

Answer [   ]

QUESTION 5

Study the following grids for 10 seconds only. Then turn the page and decide from the four options available which grid contains the collective group of coloured squares from the grids.

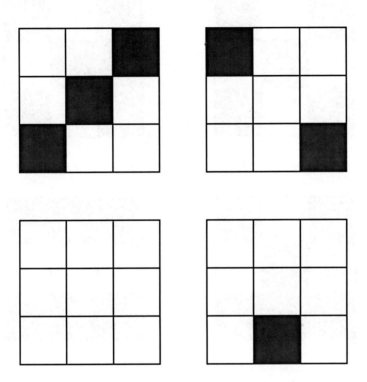

QUESTION 5 OPTIONS

A

B

C

D

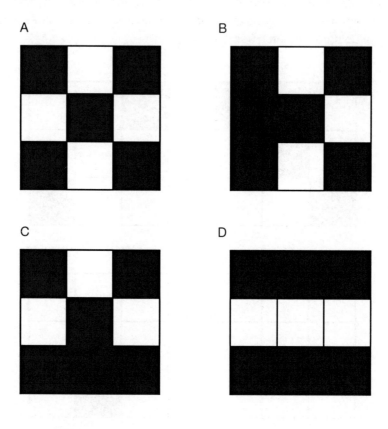

Answer

QUESTION 6

Study the following grids for 10 seconds only. Then turn the page and decide from the four options available which grid contains the collective group of coloured squares from the grids.

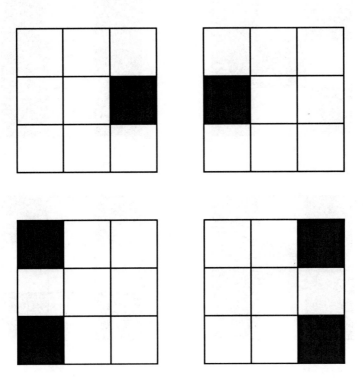

QUESTION 6 OPTIONS

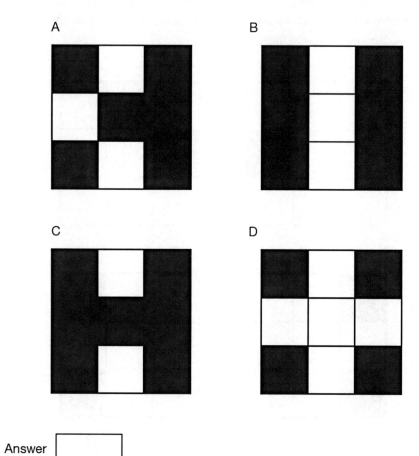

A

B

C

D

Answer

QUESTION 7

Study the following grids for 10 seconds only. Then turn the page and decide from the four options available which grid contains the collective group of coloured squares from the grids.

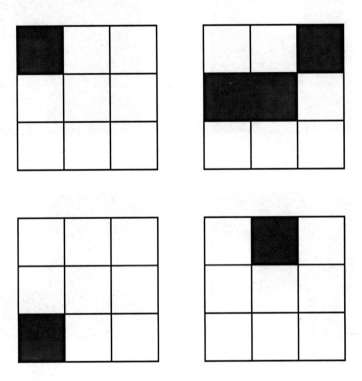

QUESTION 7 OPTIONS

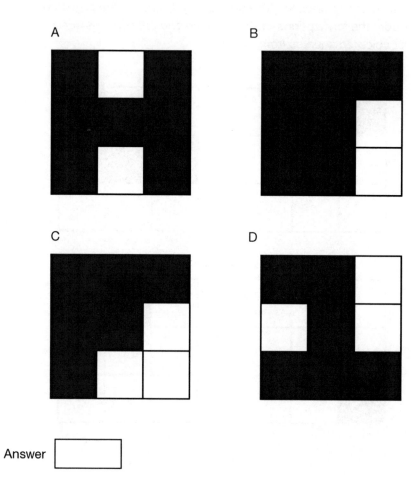

A

B

C

D

Answer

QUESTION 8

Study the following grids for 10 seconds only. Then turn the page and decide from the four options available which grid contains the collective group of coloured squares from the grids.

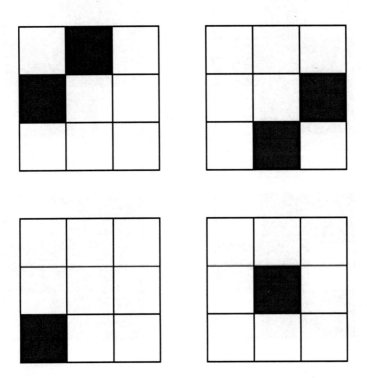

QUESTION 8 OPTIONS

A

B

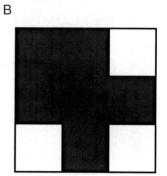

C

D

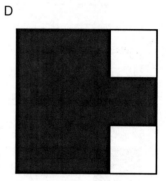

Answer _____

QUESTION 9

Study the following grids for 10 seconds only. Then turn the page and decide from the four options available which grid contains the collective group of coloured squares from the grids.

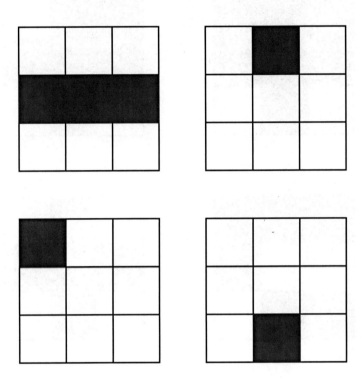

QUESTION 9 OPTIONS

A

B

C

D

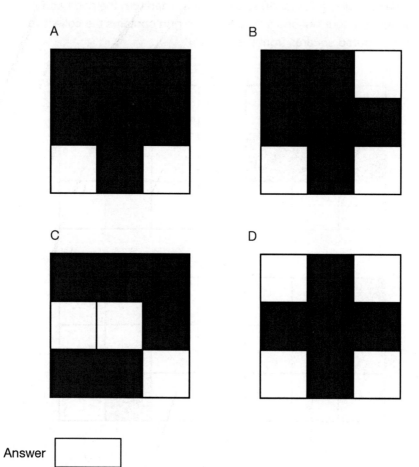

Answer

QUESTION 10

Study the following grids for 10 seconds only. Then turn the page and decide from the four options available which grid contains the collective group of coloured squares from the grids.

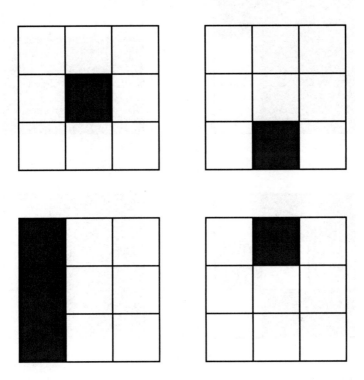

QUESTION 10 OPTIONS

A

B

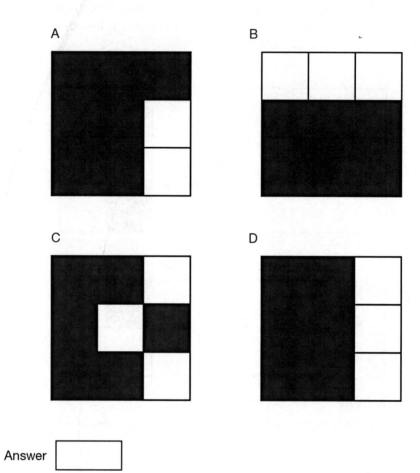

C

D

Answer

ANSWERS TO MEMORY TEST PART 2

1. B

2. A

3. A

4. D

5. C

6. B

7. C

8. A

9. B

10. D

OVERCOMING TEST NERVES

The majority of people who are required to undertake any form of test will get nervous. This is only natural and without some degree of nerves you won't be able to perform to the best of your ability. However, some people will unfortunately experience uncontrollable nerves. It is only natural to feel nervous before test but there are a number of things that you can do to get over these nerves. To begin with, lets take a look at a few of the more common pre-test anxieties:

- Feeling generally nervous and anxious
- Sweaty hands and palms
- Trembling voice
- Sore head
- Aching muscles
- Dry mouth
- Increased heart beat
- Shaky hands

I can remember taking my driving test at the age of 17 and feeling a few of the above symptoms. In the build up to the test I had worried myself so much that eventually I thought, "What's the point in all of this? It's only a driving test, who cares if I fail?" I had seriously reached the point where I didn't really care anymore whether I passed or failed. Now this is probably going to sound stupid, but this change in attitude actually worked in my favour. I performed a lot better during the driving test, simply because inside I had stopped caring, and therefore the nerves went out of the window. Now I am not saying that you shouldn't care about your tests, because that would be silly. But what I am saying is that you can only do so much practice and you can only do so many mock tests. Once you have done sufficient preparation for the tests, and you will know when that time has come, then it is pointless worrying anymore about it. Do your study, do your preparation, and then go to the test centre feeling free, calm and relaxed, and trust me, you will perform a whole lot better!

VISUALISING THE TEST BEFORE YOU ATTEND IT

This is a great method that works for many people. Before you attend the test, try and visualise the entire process. Sit down in your favourite armchair and close your eyes. Think about driving to the test centre with plenty of time to spare. You arrive early at the venue and sit in the car park composing yourself and reading through a number of sample test questions. When you walk into the test centre you are standing tall, smiling and feeling relaxed and confident. You introduce yourself in a polite manner and shake the hands of the assessor. You sit down in the chair and listen carefully to all instructions. Once the test commences you work quickly, yet calmly, and you try your hardest to answer all of the questions accurately. Once you have completed the test you take the time to go back through your answers.

The above method is a fantastic way of focusing yourself prior to any test. If you try to visualise the entire process being successful before the event starts, then this will put you in the correct frame of mind.

ALTERNATIVE TESTING RESOURCES

I hope that you have found this guide to be a great use in your preparation for the RAF Test. You can also obtain further testing resources from the website WWW.HOW2BECOME.COM including sample online testing questions.

I also have available an **ARMED FORCES TESTS** book which you can buy on Amazon – just search for 'Richard McMunn' on Amazon to see my full range of books. Good luck!

how2become

Visit www.how2become.com to find more titles and courses that will help you to pass any job interview or selection process:

- Online Armed forces testing

- Job interview DVDs and books

- 1-day intensive career training courses

- Psychometric testing books and CDs.

www.how2become.com